P9-CFC-662

GROWING

TOWARD

SPIRITUAL

MATURITY

Box 327, 110 Bridge Street
Wheaton, Illinois 60189

First Edition
9 8 7 6
0 9 8 7 6 5 4 3
ISBN: 0-910566-45-3

©1988 by Evangelical Training Association. All rights reserved. Printed in the United States of America. No part of this book may be used or reproduced in any manner whatsoever without written permission except in the case of brief quotations with credit embodied in articles, books, and reviews. For information, write Evangelical Training Association, P.O. Box 327, Wheaton, IL 60189.

CONTENTS

INTRODUCTION

The moment you invite Christ into your life and experience conversion, a monumental change takes place. Your life is never the same. The extent of that change, however, depends upon how much you seek, allow, and foster growth in your spiritual life. That spiritual growth is never automatic. It can be carelessly left to chance or carefully planned and cultivated. This course is committed to the latter.

In developing this text the Association has brought together the following individuals and wishes to express gratitude for contributing chapters to this text:

Dr. Burt D. Braunius

Dr. Kermit A. Ecklebarger

Dr. Paul J. Loth

Dr. Gary C. Newton

Dr. Richard Patterson

Dr. Arthur M. Ross

The purpose of bringing together a seminary professor, a Bible college professor, a Christian university professor, an adult educator, a correspondence school dean, and an organizational executive was to stimulate your thinking and response in as wide a scope as possible. The intent is to expose you to the best in biblical thought by a cross-section of evangelical leaders on how to grow spiritually and live for Christ.

The title, *Growing Toward Spiritual Maturity*, was deliberately chosen to emphasize that your spiritual growth will not be completed until you meet your Savior and are changed into his glorious design (I John 3:2).

As you embark upon this study, consider what Martin Luther said many years ago about spiritual growth. He said that three things would work against your spiritual growth—the world, Satan, and yourself.

Though it is tempting to think of growth as natural, sure, and automatic (which may be true biologically), it is not true spiritually. Growth is a struggle. This may seem discouraging as you begin a training experience in spiritual growth. However, spiritual growth is sometimes difficult and always demanding.

5

It sometimes seems as if the entire world works against your growth. Romans 8:22 speaks of this struggle in eloquent terms. The world is not waiting with open arms to assist you in your growth pilgrimage. The world is in sin and struggles against every Christian with determined resistance.

Satan works against you in this endeavor as well. Job's experience shows that Satan has access to God to indict, criticize, and condemn believers. Scripture pictures him as a roaring lion seeking whom he may devour and destroy. Thus in spiritual growth, it is essential to reconfirm that Satan is in this world and that he is a formidable foe.

Of course, one major battle will always be self. Even the apostle Paul knew this struggle intensely (Rom. 7:23-25). Paul did not describe growth as a skirmish or a challenge; he carefully chose the term "war."

Therefore, regardless of how long you have been a believer, whether a day or many decades, growing in Christ is necessary, fulfilling, and satisfying, but always a struggle. Growth is the target, as Paul has exhorted in II Cor. 7:1.

We, like the coliseum spectators watching the gladiators of old, cheer you on to that level of spiritual growth that brings full joy and glory to the Lord.

YOUR FOUNDATION FOR SPIRITUAL GROWTH

BEING PART OF
GOD'S FAMILY

1 Healthy Christians are spiritually-growing Christians. Growth is as normal and necessary for the Christian life as for the physical body. Entering God's family by new birth, believers become "babes in Christ" (I Cor. 3:1). Whether fifteen or fifty, new Christians begin as spiritual infants needing to "grow up" in their salvation (I Pet. 2:2 NIV). God wants and expects these newborn Christians to grow. To help them in this maturing process he provides gifted leaders (Eph. 4:11-14). This is made evident in Colossians where Paul says that one of his goals was to "present every man perfect (mature) in Christ Jesus" (Col. 1:28).

Unfortunately, growing spiritually is not automatic. In spite of God's desire and provision for growth, some believers never grow up. This problem of stunted spiritual growth is not new. It harmed two New Testament congregations. Tension between believers at Corinth forced Paul to continue feeding them a milk diet suitable for "babes in Christ" at a time when they should have been ready for solid spiritual food (I Cor. 3:1,2). Other believers mentioned in Hebrews had been Christians long enough to be teachers, but they still needed to be taught basic Christian truths (Heb. 5:12).

Why don't Christians grow? There are a variety of reasons. Sometimes believers are misinformed. Groups which only emphasize evangelism often imply that the salvation experience is all that is needed. Maturity automatically comes with conversion. Viewing new birth as an end in itself stifles incentive for maturing as a Christian.

A desire for instant spirituality keeps others from developing into strong believers. Many search for some simple formula for instant godliness. They crave some spiritual experience that will produce effortless and victorious Christian living. These people fail because they are looking in the wrong place. Growing spiritually is a lifelong experience. Even the apostle Paul confessed that he had not "already attained, either were already perfect" (Phil. 3:12). When Paul said this, he had been a Christian at least twenty-five years, had completed three missionary journeys, and written nine of the New Testament epistles. Three verses later Paul includes himself among those who are "mature," but he knew that maturity was never absolute. Christian living is a dynamic experience in growing spiritually throughout life.

Maturing in Christ involves many things. Like physical fitness, it includes proper nourishment, adequate exercise, good hygiene, and a positive outlook. Spiritual fitness results from feeding on God's Word (John 6:26,27,63), developing strength of character by prayerfully persevering through the hard experiences of life (James 1:2-5), being sensitive to and dealing with sin (I John 1:9), and expecting victory over temptation because of the finished work of Christ (I Cor. 10:13).

Since growth is essential to healthy Christian living and since it is not automatic, believers must maintain a balanced spiritual fitness program. Like heart disease, spiritual immaturity is very deceptive. Those who have it often don't know it. The believers at Corinth thought they were mature (I Cor. 3:18-21; 4:8-10). But a fuller understanding of what it means to be a part of God's family would have helped them to avoid spiritual immaturity. The more Christians understand the new birth and the lordship of Christ, the better they will appreciate the spiritual resources available to them as God's children.

■ Understanding the new birth ■

Becoming part of God's family starts with the new birth. When Jesus told Nicodemus, a religious leader, "Except a man be born again, he cannot see the kingdom of God" (John 3:3), he meant that everyone must experience a new beginning. Just as personal life starts with physical birth, so reception into God's family requires a spiritual origin. God gives a new kind of life, eternal life, to those who place their faith in Jesus (John 3:16). The inner life is renewed spiritually by the Spirit of God (John 3:5,6). It is as if the person had been created all over again (II Cor. 5:17). The believer enjoys the new quality of life that is a part of the new order brought by Jesus. This new life not only qualifies people for heaven, it also prepares them to experience the more abundant life in Jesus now (John 10:10). New birth brings growth-enabling changes.

New family relationships

New birth brings new family relationships. Believers become a part of "the household of God" (Eph. 2:19). Paul reminds his Gentile readers that these new family ties are a special privilege. Formerly they were not part of God's chosen people Israel, had not received his salvation message directly, and, most seriously, were without "hope and without God in the world" (Eph. 2:11,12). God has taken the initiative through the death of Christ to remove the barriers separating people from people and people from God. Appreciating this new family status gives believers a sense of personal significance. They are important to God.

Through the new birth believers receive a new parent. God becomes their father. Indeed, as creator, God fathered all people; but sin severed those family ties (John 8:44). The new birth restores that father-child relationship with God. Those who trust Jesus receive the "right to become children of God" (John 1:12 NIV). At the new birth God sends the Holy Spirit into believers' lives, assuring them that they are his adopted children (Gal. 4:5,6). This "Spirit of sonship" enables them to naturally call out to him, "Abba, Father," the same affectionate words Jesus used during his hour of trial (Mark 14:36).

With God as their father, believers rest secure in divine love. They receive love that transcends human understanding and from which nothing can separate them (Eph. 3:18,19; Rom. 8:35-39). True to this deep love, the heavenly father disciplines his children to produce correction and growth (Heb. 12:6). But, because he is a forgiving father, repentant, errant children can draw near with confidence (I John 1:9-2:2). Knowing that every hard experience of life is filtered by God's infinite wisdom and fatherly love, Christians can face difficulties with renewed assurance. What God allows is always for his glory and our growth (James 1:2-4).

New family support also comes from new brothers and sisters in Christ. The spiritual family includes all who trust Jesus (Gal. 6:10). Fellow believers should provide a supportive caring community that stimulates growth (I Cor. 12:25; Eph. 4:11-16). God did not plan Christian living as a solitary existence. Believers need each other. From the beginning, Christians have met for instruction, fellowship, celebrating communion, and prayer (Acts 2:42). God has given gifted teachers to the church to supplement personal Bible study, thus promoting growth through a better knowledge of God's Word (Eph. 4:14). Mature believers learn how to apply biblical truth to everyday life (Heb. 5:13,14). As the Christian community gets acquainted through fellowship, opportunities for compassionate support arise (I Cor 12:26). Through corporate worship, believers stimulate each other's faith. Above all, family relationships among God's children are to be marked by brotherly love and hospitality (Rom. 12:10-13; Heb. 13:1). Christ's sacrificial love sets the standard for believers' unselfish love to each other. True Christians are known by their love (John 13:34,35).

Living in God's family cultivates growth. Believers experience healthy self-esteem as they discover that others need them. Each believer has an essential and important contribution to make to the well-being of the community (I Cor. 12:14-20). Yet, because each believer needs the gifts of others for personal growth, mutual dependence develops (I Cor. 12:21-25). Believers grow by giving and receiving help.

New heavenly citizenship

New birth brings a change of citizenship. Former foreigners and aliens become "fellow citizens with the saints" (Eph. 2:19). Believers now enjoy all the rights and privileges of heavenly citizenship. But this new allegiance creates a problem. Continuing to be resident of this world, God's people face the tensions that come with living in a foreign country. Suddenly those who "fit in" before because they belonged to this world find that they are not as well received (John 15:19). Believers face the challenge of being "in the world" but "not of the world" (John 17:11,14). Their former home becomes their mission as they seek to win others to Jesus (John 17:18).

When Paul reminded the believers at Philippi that they should live like citizens of heaven, his first century readers knew well what he meant. Philippi was a Roman colony. Colonial status conferred Roman citizenship on those born there. City government operated like a miniature Rome. Although they lived hundreds of miles from the imperial city, a journey of over a month, they lived like Romans with full rights of Roman citizenship. These believers knew what it was to live like citizens of a far-away place. They could easily identify with living consistent with one's heavenly homeland. Believers must live as responsible, law-abiding members of their earthly communities without compromising their loyalty to God (Rom. 13:1-7). New birth implants a hope of heaven (I Pet. 1:4). Eagerly anticipating their heavenly home helps believers keep a proper sense of priorities (Phil. 3:17-21).

This perspective of heavenly citizenship contributes greatly to growing spiritually. Life away from our heavenly home is not always easy. How can God's people keep from losing heart under these pressures? Although they may be perishing outwardly, inwardly they are "renewed day by day" (II Cor. 4:16-18). By viewing things from the perspective of their heavenly citizenship, believers see the temporary nature of their troubles in contrast to the eternal blessing awaiting in that unseen world. Heavenly-oriented living promotes mature Christian living.

New inheritance

Newborn members of God's family share fully in a large inheritance. There is nothing uncertain about this bequest. God both preserves the inheritance and protects the heirs. At the second coming of Christ, the believer will receive these spiritual possessions now stored in heaven (I Pet. 1:3-5). More remarkable than the size or certainty of this inheritance is the fact it is not entirely future. At the new birth believers already receive part of it. The Holy Spirit received at the time of the new birth "is a deposit guaranteeing our inheritance until the redemption of those who are God's possession" (Eph. 1:14 NIV). Like a down payment, the Spirit insures the full inheritance at Christ's coming (II Cor. 5:5 NIV).

As the foretaste of future heavenly blessings, the Spirit produces the fruits of "love, joy, peace, longsuffering, gentleness, goodness, faith, meekness" and "temperance" in the Christian life (Gal. 5:22,23). These qualities come as believers are "filled with the Spirit" which means to allow the Spirit, not the desires of the flesh, to influence one's behavior. This Spirit-filled life manifests itself in corporate praise, inward joy, continual thanksgiving, and harmonious relationships with other Christians through mutual submission (Eph. 5:18-21). Growing up as a Christian requires tapping the resource of the Spirit in daily living. Ephesians 5:18-21 tells how one is to be filled with the Spirit, not just what the results will be. Paul wrote these four verses as only one sentence. The following diagram brings out Paul's point:

And be not drunk with wine
  wherein is excess,
but be filled with the Spirit
  by speaking to yourselves in psalms, hymns and spiritual songs
  by singing and making melody in your heart to the Lord
  by giving thanks always for all things in the name of our Lord
    Jesus Christ
  by submitting yourselves one to another in the fear of God

Since Paul commands several of these responses elsewhere, it is likely that he teaches believers how to release the Spirit's control in their lives (I Thess. 5:18; Phil. 4:4-6; Col. 3:16,17). As one responds in obedience in these areas, the Spirit produces the right attitude.

■ The Lordship of Christ ■

The confession, "Jesus is Lord," was possibly the first creed recited by the early church. This phrase may have been a part of Christian baptism in New Testament times (Acts 8:16; 19:5). As a messianic title for the ascended Jesus, "Lord" was a key point in Peter's Pentecost sermon (Acts 2:36), the celebration of Christ's humility in Phil. 2:6-11 (possibly an early church hymn quoted here by Paul), and the public profession of faith by new converts (Rom. 10:9,10). Nothing more highly emphasizes the importance of calling Jesus Lord than its use as the test for exposing evil spirits (I Cor. 12:3).

Being one of the most frequently used words in the New Testament, "lord" reflects a wide range of meanings in its 717 occurrences. In the ancient Roman world "lord" was a greeting meaning "sir," an expression of respect for a teacher, an acknowledgement of submission by a slave to his owner, a title of honor for a king, and a title of worship for God. All of these meanings occurred concerning Jesus, but the last four directly relate to growing spiritually within God's family. To become a Christian you must "confess with your mouth, 'Jesus is Lord,' and believe in your heart that God raised him from the dead" (Rom. 10:9 NIV). Since Paul clearly teaches that salvation is by faith alone (Eph. 2:8,9), recognizing Jesus as Lord is not an additional requirement. Rather, it is a part of saving faith. To trust Jesus is to trust him as Lord. Faith is an attitude of reliance and commitment that comes from realizing that Jesus is Lord. Trusting in Jesus as Lord includes several growth-producing attitudes.

Obeying Jesus as teacher
Trusting Jesus as Lord involves accepting him as an authoritative teacher. Spiritual stability comes to those who base their lives on his teaching. Those who ignore his teaching do so at their own peril (Matt. 7:21-28). Following the feeding of the 5,000, many of Jesus' disciples became disillusioned by his "bread of life" teaching and ceased following him. When he asked the apostles if they wanted to leave too, Peter responded, "Lord, to whom shall we go? thou hast the words of eternal life" (John

6:68). To recognize Jesus as Lord is to accept the truthfulness and absolute necessity of his message for salvation.

Such confidence that his teachings are true naturally leads to obedience. The greatest inconsistency is to call Jesus "Lord" while disregarding his instructions. With penetrating conviction Jesus asks, "Why do ye call me Lord, Lord, and do not the things which I say?" (Luke 6:46). Acknowledging Jesus as Lord involves being a disciple who accepts and lives by Jesus' teaching, not just a pupil who is intrigued with his thought. Only those who accept Jesus the teacher as Lord by living according to his teaching experience the liberating freedom that life based on truth brings (John 8:31,32).

Serving Jesus as slave owner

A most common use of "lord" in the ancient biblical world was as the title for a slave owner. Roman law gave absolute control to the master over his slaves. They were his possessions to do with as he pleased. While most masters were relatively good to their slaves, they were still possessions and thereby had no rights. Accordingly, when believers called themselves "servants of Christ Jesus," they were indicating their absolute submission to Christ who owned them (Rom. 1:1; Phil. 1:1; II Tim 2:24). Christ, their master, had the right to totally rule every aspect of their lives. Paul reminds believers that they owe Christ complete obedience because they are not their own. They have been "bought with a price" (I Cor. 6:20; 7:23). "Lord" is not merely a pious-sounding phrase for worship, but an attitude of commitment for daily living. Thus believers are to serve the Lord as slaves (Rom. 12:11).

Granting Christ this complete control over one's life is not something optional in the Christian life. Making him Lord does not make a believer a super-spiritual person. It is not going the extra mile. Normal Christian living treats him as Lord. Anything less is sin. He is Lord because he purchased us by his death. That is an objective fact. Responding to him as Lord is a lifelong relationship. Progressively throughout life Christ makes new claims upon our obedience by which we reconfirm our submission to his authority over us.

But Christ's ownership means much more than just duty to perform. Having Christ as master is a great blessing that makes spiritual growth possible. Salvation involves a change of masters. Formerly Satan and sin controlled the person's life like an evil slave master. By faith in Christ the believer has been made free from slavery to sin (Rom. 6:17,18). No longer enslaved by Satan, the believer is free to serve Christ. Although Satan continues to tempt us, his control has been broken. Christ bought us at the slave market, freeing us to serve God (Gal. 5:1; Rom. 6:22). Knowing that slavery to sin has been broken by Christ gives the believer growth expectancy.

Honoring Jesus as king

The term "lord" also belonged to the language of the palace. This was a title of honor suitable for the reigning king. To address the king as "lord" showed respect for his sovereign reign. Contemporaries of Jesus who knew that he was the promised messianic ruler hailed him, "O Lord, *thou* Son of David" (Matt. 15:22; 20:30,31). The early church especially used the title "Lord" to indicate the sovereign reign of the ascended Christ at God's right hand. Eventually every knee will bow before Jesus and every person will "confess that Jesus Christ is Lord" (Phil 2:10,11). Jesus who now reigns in exile from heaven ultimately will be recognized as King of the world (I Cor. 15:24-28).

Christians who are growing spiritually live as loyal subjects to their reigning Lord. He alone is king of their lives. Along with this responsibility of citizenship, comes the encouragement of knowing his royal power. Jesus' Great Commission to be witnesses to the whole world was reinforced with the promise, "All power is given unto me in heaven and in earth" (Matt. 28:18-20). The task is gigantic, but the resources of the king of the universe are more than adequate.

Worshiping Jesus as God

Most important of all, when Christians called Jesus "Lord," they were claiming that he was God. By New Testament times the Jews had developed such a respect for God's holiness that they avoided saying his personal name "Jehovah." Whenever possible they substituted a Hebrew title meaning "Lord." In translating the Old Testament into Greek, the word "Lord" was used 6,156 times to replace "Jehovah." "Lord" was a title that belonged especially to God. It stood for God's highest name. To confess "Jesus is Lord" is to call him God. All that God is, Jesus is (John 20:28). Familiarity with him as friend must never distract from that sense of awe and wonder in his presence. Jesus is the object of worship deserving total praise and adoration. But again, duty gives rise to growth. True worship builds character and consistent character produces effective service (I Tim. 3:14-16; 4:8,15,16).

The lordship of Christ is a big concept. The better believers honor Jesus as God, as reigning king, as master, and as teacher, the more mature they will be in Christian living.

■ Summary ■

An important goal for all Christians is spiritual maturity. Reaching spiritual maturity is a lengthy and ongoing process whereby you grow toward a deeper understanding of the Christian life and Christ himself. The first step in the process of spiritual growth is understanding the beginning of the new life in Christ, "the new birth." You must realize that you now have a new family with whom to relate, a new citizenship which must be respected, and a new inheritance to enjoy.

Another important element in the process of spiritual growth is the recognition of Christ as "Lord" in every aspect of your life. The meanings of the title "Lord" as teacher, master, king, and God demonstrate the prime importance that you must put on Christ in your new life. Christ must become the teacher from whom you learn the lessons of spiritual growth. Christ must also be regarded as your master to whom you owe strict obedience. Christ must be revered as king and given total loyalty. Finally, you must acknowledge Christ's oneness with God and worship him as such. The recognition of Christ's lordship will lead you toward a deeper understanding of the concept of spiritual maturity.

■ Discussion Questions ■

1. Discuss what is meant by Christian growth and why it is important.
2. What are two main reasons why some Christians don't grow?
3. List four important aspects of a good spiritual fitness program.
4. Name three family-type benefits that result from new birth and state how each contributes to growing spiritually.
5. In what four different ways is Jesus Lord? Identify the responsibility and resource which each brings to Christian living.

■ Application Activities ■

1. Look up the phrases "new birth," "son," or "child of God," "adoption," "inheritance," and "citizen" in a Bible dictionary to see how these ideas are used in the Bible.
2. Look up the word "lord" in a Bible concordance. On four separate sheets of paper, each titled with one of the following headings, list the Bible reference every time it is used: (1) clearly of God, (2) specifically of Jesus, (3) either of Jesus or God without clear distinction, and (4) of someone other than God or Jesus. After each reference, write a brief summary of the passage showing the main theme of the verses where "lord" is used. When you finish, study each of the four pages to see how lord is used concerning God, Jesus, either, and others. What insights are learned for living with Jesus as your "Lord?"

■ Bibliography ■

Grounds, Vernon. *Radical Commitment: Getting Serious About Christian Growth*. Portland, OR: Multnomah Press, 1984.

MacDonald, Gordon. *Ordering Your Private World*. Nashville: Thomas Nelson Publishers, 1985.

Tenney, Merrill C. *Roads a Christian Must Travel*. Wheaton, IL: Tyndale House Publishers, Inc., 1979.

SOURCE OF
CHRISTIAN LIVING

2 Membership in God's family begins with the new birth followed by a lifelong adventure in spiritual growth. Reading and studying God's Word provides the nourishment necessary for this growth (I Pet. 2:2). Furthermore, the privilege of belonging to God's family carries the obligation of living as a responsible family member. As God's Word, the Bible both describes the kind of life that God's children should live and provides the resources for consistent Christian living.

■ The Bible as God's Word ■

The Bible repeatedly claims to be God's Word. More than 760 times in the Old Testament the authors identify their messages as "the word of God" or some equivalent phrase. Hundreds of statements, especially in the Prophets, begin with some form of the expression "the Lord saith" (e.g. Jer. 31:1-40). During his earthly ministry, Jesus endorsed all three sections of the Hebrew Bible, the Law, the Prophets, and the Writings (Luke 24:44) and emphasized the divine origin of the Old Testament (Mark 7:7,8).

The New Testament also claims to be God's Word. Jesus proclaimed his own gospel message with such divine authority (Matt. 7:28,29) that one astonished audience exclaimed, "Never man spake like this man" (John 7:46). Insisting that God was the source of his message, Jesus said, "I do nothing of myself; but as my Father hath taught me, I speak these things" (John 8:28). The apostles also recognized the divine origin of their message and writings. Commending the Thessalonian believers, Paul wrote, "when ye received the word of God which ye heard of us, ye received it not as the word of men, but as it is in truth, the word of God" (I Thess. 2:13). Peter even gave Paul's epistles a scriptural status equal to the Old Testament (II Pet. 3:16).

The Bible clearly claims to be God's Word. That claim is verified by Jesus who demonstrated his own divine nature and trustworthiness by his sinless living, miracles, fulfillment of Old Testament prophecy, and, most of all, by his resurrection from the dead.

The authority of God's Word

Because the Bible is God's Word, it demands serious attention and respect. Several terms explain the nature of this divine authority. Biblical revelation refers to the fact that God has taken the initiative to disclose information about his nature, eternal purposes, and provision of salvation in the words of Scripture. Much of this truth was not available apart from God's own communication of it (I Cor. 2:6-12).

Biblical *inspiration* means that the Holy Spirit supernaturally controlled and guided the human authors of the biblical books so that they wrote precisely what God wanted said. As the human authors wrote from the background of their own experiences, using their minds and individual writing styles, they "spoke from God as they were carried along by the Holy Spirit" (II Pet. 1:21 NIV). God's authorship of Scripture is not limited to passages where he is the direct speaker or dictated the contents. "All Scripture is given by inspiration of God" (II Tim. 3:16). Even the choice of individual words was divinely controlled so that the terms used would convey the right meaning.

Biblical *infallibility* refers to the effectiveness of God's Word in achieving God's intended purposes (Isa. 55:11). God so works through the biblical message that his intentions are accomplished.

Biblical *inerrancy* is a technical phrase for the accuracy of the biblical message. It affirms that what the Bible teaches on any subject it addresses is true. Properly understood, the message of the Bible gives correct information.

Ultimately, the authority of God's Word focuses on personal accountability. God enforces his message (Heb. 2:1-4). Growing spiritually requires responding to the biblical message with undivided attention, humble submission, and unqualified obedience (James 1:19-22).

The unity of God's Word

Although the Bible contains 66 different books written over a period of approximately 1,500 years, it holds together as the ongoing story of God's redemptive program in the world. The Old Testament focuses primarily on God's dealing with his people Israel. The New Testament continues the story with the founding of the church, a group composed of believers in Jesus from every nation. This new institution replaced the nation Israel as the earthly manifestation of God's people. These changes do not represent a break with the past. A continuity of promise and fulfillment links the two Testaments (Matt. 5:17). The future age of spiritual blessing predicted by the prophets has begun with the ministry of Jesus (Luke 4:16-21). Even the Gentile outreach of the church is the achievement of God's initial promise to Abraham, "in thee shall all families of the earth be blessed" (Gen. 12:3 with Gal. 3:8).

Consequently, believers are biblical Christians, not just New Testament Christians. Insights for spiritual growth and Christian living come from the whole Bible (Rom. 15:4; I Cor. 10:6-11). God's supernatural control insures a coherent, non-contradictory biblical message.

The clarity of God's Word

One does not have to be a seminary professor, or even a pastor, to know what the Bible means. Scripture was not written to confuse or conceal; but to clearly communicate God's message. God's truth was told in languages spoken in everyday life. "Setting forth the truth plainly" (II Cor. 4:2 NIV) was a conscious objective of Paul's ministry.

The growth potential of God's Word

The Bible uses several picture words from everyday life to show the great variety of ways in which God's Word advances spiritual growth. As seed, God's Word is the source of the growth (Matt. 13:1-26). Young Christians grow spiritually because they are well nourished by the food God's Word provides (I Pet. 2:2; I Tim. 4:6). Using the Bible as a mirror enables believers to evaluate the consistency of their Christian living (James 1:22-25). When Satan attacks God's people, God's Word serves as "the sword of the Spirit," that offensive weapon which defeats the enemy (Eph. 6:17). Like light illuminating a dark path, biblical principles provide guidance in daily decision making (Ps. 119:105). God's Word is a tremendous resource for Christian growth and living.

The adequacy of God's Word

After declaring the divine inspiration of Scripture, Paul makes a surprisingly bold statement in II Tim. 3:16,17. The purpose of God's Word is "that the man of God may be perfect, thoroughly furnished unto all good works." Paul insists that biblical truth is adequate to totally equip believers for mature living. Scripture provides everything believers need to know to be all they ought to be in every situation.

◼ Reading for Application ◼

Knowing how valuable God's Word is for spiritual growth as a Christian, believers should read the Bible with intense personal interest. After all, the ultimate purpose of studying Scripture is to relate biblical truth to daily living. Becoming "doers of the word, and not hearers only" (James 1:22) is helped by employing certain basic Bible reading skills.

Reading with interpretive "bifocals"

Unfortunately, many Christians suffer biblical "nearsightedness." Preoccupied with their own circumstances, they read the Bible only to gain insight for today. This approach ignores the fact that the biblical message was originally spoken to someone else. To correct this problem, people need to wear interpretive "bifocals." Looking off into the distance, they first focus on the intended meaning for the original audience. Then they take the close-up look to see what it means for people living now. God's Word will never mean to Christians living today what it could not have meant to the first recipients.

Reading for the main idea of the paragraph

Bible reading should seek to discover the main point of each paragraph. Paragraphs, not verses, are the focus of good reading. Each paragraph consists of several sentences on the same subject. The main idea of the paragraph is the central theme that holds the verses together. Having identified this main idea, the reader is able to determine how each sentence helps the author make his point. Stating the main idea of the paragraph in one concise sentence may be hard at first; but it gets easier with practice.

Modern verse divisions added in AD 1560 are both a blessing and a curse. Without them, it would be next to impossible to find a specific passage. But with them, people treat each verse as an independent unit of thought. Trying to understand a verse apart from its paragraph makes it too easy to read in one's own ideas. What the author meant by a verse is clear only when it is explained consistent with the main idea of its paragraph. A wise principle of Bible study warns: the shorter the passage interpreted, the greater the danger of error.

Reading for principles of Christian living

Reading to gain insight and strength for daily Christian living is more than just looking for promises and commands. Many of the most important lessons in Scripture are not specifically spelled out. Those that are precisely expressed often focus on a narrow situation. Reading for application tries to find relevant principles for daily living. The particular instructions for Christian living are studied to discover the general spiritual, moral, or doctrinal principle which underlies them. The resulting insight is stated as a general guideline applicable to many situations in life rather than a specific rule. Current circumstances may differ greatly from those of the original audience; but the principles which guided their conduct are still valid today. A good starting point is to look for a basic principle that is consistent with the main emphasis of the biblical author for the original readers.

Reading for relevant insights

The desire to experience instant spiritual blessing often causes people to short-cut good Bible study. Breaking Bible study up into the following four steps helps God's people to find relevant insights.

Observation focuses on what the passage says. The reader watches for all the important facts in the paragraph. Someone has well said, "If you look for nothing, you will find it every time." Most important information will be discovered by looking for the five "Ws" and an "H" used by journalists: Who? What? When? Where? Why? and How? Observing all these details is a necessary first step in correctly understanding the Bible.

Interpretation asks what the passage means. All the details observed in the passage are analyzed to discover the point which the author was trying to make. Important words, significant grammatical relationships, and relevant background information must be studied in Bible dictionaries and commentaries to find their precise meanings. The correct under-standing of the paragraph adequately accounts for all of these facts. If some information does not fit naturally with the explanation of the passage, then the interpretation needs revision.

Evaluation determines the relevance of the message for God's people living today. The whole Bible is God's Word; but there are some things in the Bible that God does not expect believers to practice today. Greeting each other with a kiss of love (I Pet. 5:14) was a common gesture of friendship in Peter's day. Today such an affectionate greeting might be misunderstood; but personal warmth can be shown without kissing. Several specific guidelines help the believer determine what is valid for today.

First, biblical statements which are universal in scope have timeless relevance. They will be expressed in general terms as true for all believers. Commands given to an individual in some specific situation usually apply only to that person. Universals will be based on Christian truth rather than cultural factors. Sometimes doctrine requires a certain quality of response and local culture determines the specific physical expression of it as in the kissing example above.

Second, promises which are conditional only apply when the condition is met.

Third, guidelines changed by later revelation no longer apply. The dietary and sacrificial regulations of the Old Testament have been removed by the finished work of Christ.

Finally, biblical examples are relevant only to the extent that they are approved or censured by the biblical authors. Just because something is recorded in the Bible does not make it right.

Application relates the relevant truth discovered by the above steps to personal Christian living. The basic question, "How then should I live?" is the constant concern. But to arrive at the answer to this question, the reader asks three questions: What spiritual principle is the author consistently impressing upon his audience which is still valid today? What is the corresponding situation in my life today? What does God expect me to do today in that corresponding situation? However, knowing what the valid principles are is not enough. To fulfill this step the reader must put them into practice in daily living.

■ Principles of Hermeneutics ■

Hermeneutics is the science of determining the correct rules to follow in interpreting the Bible. Examining how people use language to communicate ideas, hermeneutics states the principles that one must follow to correctly understand the Bible. While the main idea of most passages is clear from a simple reading of the text, others require careful thought to get the author's point (II Pet. 3:16). It is easy to twist Scripture to make it support any particular bias. Most cults are based on misinter-preted biblical passages. Careful study using correct rules is necessary to avoid distorting God's Word (II Cor. 4:2).

Studying God's Word is more necessary now than it was for the original recipients in biblical times. The Bible was originally written in foreign languages to people living a long time ago in another part of the world with a different culture. The following rules of hermenuetics help you to overcome these barriers so that you can correctly understand God's Word.

Identify the author's literary style

People do not always use words literally. When someone complains about a speaker by saying, "Did he ever dig himself into a hole!" people don't look for a ladder to help him get out. The word "hole" in this sense does not mean a pit in the ground. It is a way of saying that his argument was inconsistent. Similarly, biblical authors often use figures of speech. While the historical books and New Testament epistles were written in a fairly direct style, Old Testament prophets often used poetry just like those who composed psalms and proverbial sayings. Jesus frequently taught in parables. Each literary style uses language in special ways. Readers must understand every passage according to its distinct literary style.

Consider the flow of the biblical content

In normal conversation, people understand words and sentences according to their context. Thoughts are expressed by a series of related ideas. Accurate Bible reading requires understanding what is written according to the author's train of thought. Specific phrases and sentences must be understood consistent with the main idea of the author. The promise of wisdom in James 1:5 does not guarantee risk free decision making through prayer. Earlier in the paragraph, James tells believers to respond with joy to hardships in life because endurance of difficult experiences develops spiritual maturity. Here the promised wisdom provides insight on how to cope during the hard experience.

Understand the meaning of key words

Words express ideas; but every word can have several different meanings. The statement, "That was the largest trunk I had ever seen" can mean more than one thing. Does the trunk refer to a tree, car, elephant, suitcase, or clothing? Normally, the other ideas mentioned in the context automatically make clear which meaning the author has in mind. Similarly, when people read the Bible in a good modern language translation, the meaning of most words will be clear. Important words or unclear terms need to be looked up in a Bible dictionary to see what the possible meanings were in the biblical author's day. Often there are shades of meaning which are hard to bring out in a translation, but add much insight to the author's intended meaning. Care must be taken to pick the one best meaning for each word studied and to understand a passage in light of the words actually used by the author. Students often inappropriately claim the promise of "wisdom" in James 1:5 when they take tests. What they need is "knowledge," not "wisdom." Quoting this verse is no substitute for study.

Follow the force of the grammar
People normally communicate with a series of words. One word sentences are rare. The way words are arranged in a sentence affects meaning as much as the choice of the words. Rearranging the same words makes a big difference. To say "The man hit the ball" is quite different from "The ball hit the man." The reader must pay close attention to grammatical forms which the author used to communicate his point. Simple things like verb tense and conjunctions are important clues to meaning. Find the main statement in each sentence and then see how the author qualifies it by other phrases. When James commands his readers to "count it all joy" when they experience different kinds of adversity, he is not suggesting that they psych themselves up so that it won't seem so bad. Rather, by beginning verse 3 with the word "because," James shows the reason why believers are to respond to adversity with joy. They know that the trying of their faith produces perseverance, a much needed spiritual quality.

View from the perspective of the historical background
Reading the Bible is like reading someone else's mail. The Bible was first written to people living in another continent, during a much earlier century, and with a different culture. To understand God's message to them, the reader needs to know as much as possible about them and their circumstances. The more readers mentally put themselves back into the situation of the original audience, the better they are able to know the intended meaning of the Bible and its significance for today.

Integrate with other biblical teaching on the subject
The Bible does not say all it has to say about a subject in any one passage. Information learned in one passage should be understood in conjunction with other key verses on the same subject. Only then will the full teaching on the theme be known. Basing an action on only one verse is like "running with only one shoe on."

■ Summary ■

The main ingredient for spiritual growth is a steady diet of God's Word. The Bible contains God's instructions on how to live as his children. An important realization which you must make is that the Bible is entirely inspired of God and, as such, is the source of consistent Christian living. You must learn how to properly read the Bible by observing the focus of the passage, interpreting its meaning, and evaluating its relevance in order to apply it to your daily living. The use of hermeneutics, the science of determining the correct rules for biblical interpretation, is helpful when trying to understand God's Word as the source of Christian living.

■ Discussion Questions ■

1. What evidence is there that the Bible claims to be God's Word?
2. Discuss how biblical revelation, inspiration, infallibility, and inerrancy differ from each other. Why are they important?
3. Explain why the unity of the Bible is so surprising. Describe what holds the message of the Bible together.
4. Name and describe the five analogies which show how Scripture helps believers grow spiritually.
5. What are the five great characteristics of the Bible as God's Word?
6. List and explain the four things that one should focus on in reading the Bible for application.
7. Name and define the four steps that should be followed in reading for relevant insights. Why should these steps be in this order?
8. Why are rules necessary for Bible study?
9. List and explain the six principles of hermeneutics.

■ Application Activities ■

1. Read the first chapter of James and note the main idea of each paragraph in a separate sentence. The paragraphs are verses 2-8, 9-11, 12, 13-15, 16-18, 19-21, 22-26, and 26-27. Later do all of James.
2. Study James 1:2-8 following the four steps: observation, interpretation, evaluation, and application. Write each of these four words on the top of a separate sheet of paper. List the questions which apply to each step on the appropriate page and then record everything important which you find as you do each step in sequence.
3. Reviewing the above page titled, "interpretation," write how each of the six principles of hermeneutics support your conclusion.

■ Bibliography ■

Fee, Gordon D. and Stuart, Douglas. *How to Read the Bible for All Its Worth*. Grand Rapids: Zondervan Pub. House, 1982.

Mickelsen, Berkeley A. and Alvera M. *Understanding Scripture*. Ventura, CA: Regal Books, 1982.

Sterrett, T. Norton. *How to Understand Your Bible*. Downers Grove, IL: InterVarsity Press, 1974.

COMMUNICATION
WITH GOD

3 In the Bible God speaks to his people. Through prayer believers talk with him. Few people ever have opportunity to speak personally with the leader of their nation, yet believers are privileged to talk to the highest being in the universe at any-time. Unlimited access into God's presence has been secured by Christ's death, resurrection, and ascension (Heb. 4:14-16; Eph. 1:18). By his actions and words God has shown that he is warm and personal, not a cold impersonal force. Encouraged by God's fatherly love, common people can confidently speak to the infinite God. Talking with his Father was a regular part of Jesus' earthly life. If prayer was essential to the God-man, how much more necessary it is for humans. Assuring them that their heavenly Father cares, Christ urges people to pray (Matt. 7:7-11).

■ Reasons for prayer ■

But why pray? Since God is all-knowing, all-powerful, and all-loving, what purpose does prayer serve? Certainly, prayer is not needed to inform God about personal circumstances. God knows what his people need before they ask (Matt. 6:32). Likewise, it is not necessary for people to try to change God's attitude toward them. God is not a cosmic bully intent on harming people. Although pagan prayers often were designed to appease a hostile deity, the true God does not desire this (Matt 6:25-34). After all, God gives only good gifts (James 1:17).

Furthermore, prayer is not talking God into something that he doesn't want to do. The Christian's proper attitude in prayer is submission to God's will, not achieving his/her own (Matt. 6:10). Jesus' triple prayer as he awaited his impending crucifixion makes this clear, "O my Father, if it be possible, let this cup pass from me: nevertheless not as I will, but as thou wilt" (Matt. 26:39-44). The believer's assurance in prayer is, "if we ask any thing according to his will, he heareth us" (I John 5:14).

The purpose of prayer is not to change God's mind. Rather, it is to align one's will with God's will. Passages where God appears to modify his stated plans in response to prayer probably were learning experiences designed by God to teach valuable lessons to his children (Gen. 18:16-33).

24

Finally, the reason for prayer is not to experience some mystical union with God. Persons praying do not loose their individual identity by becoming one with God as eastern religions claim. Prayer is an intimate relationship between two parties, not one person becoming aware that he really is a part of the other. Indeed, there is a spiritual element to prayer. People sense the presence of God who is always there.

If prayer does not do any of these things, it seems like a complete waste of time and effort! Why pray? Because God has willed to work in answer to prayer. Prayer makes a difference. "The effectual fervent prayer of a righteous man availeth much" (James 5:16). In his infinite wisdom, God made prayer an important part of his program. Through prayer believers have a cooperative role in God's involvement in human affairs.

Someone has well said, "Prayer is for our benefit, not God's." Being sovereign over everyone and everything that exists, God didn't need human prayer to accomplish his eternal purposes. The reason for prayer is our weak, vulnerable humanity. Because people have a terrible tendency to ignore God, prayer stimulates loyalty by reminding them of their dependence upon God. It also contributes to growing spiritually.

■ A balanced prayer life ■

Since prayer is so vital to spiritual maturity and a healthy relationship with God, it is necessary that the following experiences be included in a balanced prayer life.

Worship

Entering God's presence should impress believers with his worth. A sense of awe and reverence is the natural response to the presence of the greatest being there is. When believers meditate on who God is, a feeling of esteem for God fills their hearts. By concentrating on the perfection of God's being, believers clear their minds of the clutter from daily life that distracts them from sensing God's presence. Because God is spirit, he desires that his children worship him "in spirit and in truth" (John 4:23,24). God must be valued above all else as you approach him in prayer.

Confession

Recognition of God's holiness naturally leaves people with a sense of sinfulness requiring confession. Experiencing how utterly holy God is, the prophet Isaiah cried out, "Woe is me! for I am undone; because I am a man of unclean lips, and I dwell in the midst of a people of unclean lips: for mine eyes have seen the King, the Lord of hosts" (Isa. 6:5). Every believer needs this cleansing that comes from acknowledging guilt. "If we confess our sins, he is faithful and just to forgive us our sins, and to cleanse us from all unrighteousness" (I John 1:9). This means that God is absolutely right in forgiving sin every time believers truly confess. People often stop growing spiritually because they fail to accept God's forgiveness. A healthy prayer life is an antidote to spiritual paralysis.

Adoration

Reassured by the loving forgiveness of the heavenly Father (I John 4:10), believers need to tell God how much they love him. An atmosphere of adoration and affectionate warmth marks a good prayer time. Expressing love to God by word and obedient actions is the only appropriate response to one who loves believers so much (I John 3:1; 4:16). Jesus taught that your first responsibility is to love God with your whole being (Matt. 22:37). This love is no empty sentimental gesture. It reflects the resolve of the will as well as emotional feelings.

Praise

Whereas worship appreciates who God is, praise pays tribute to what God does. He deserves praise "for his mighty acts . . . according to his excellent greatness" (Ps. 150:2). Believers should speak highly of his great goodness and gracious compassion (Ps. 145:4,5). Because "the Lord is good to all, and His tender mercies are over all his works" (Ps. 145:9). God is honored and Christians grow when they credit Him. Praise projects a positive outlook on life by remembering God's favors.

Thanksgiving

No aspect of prayer is more essential than thanksgiving. Having received God's forgiving grace and sustaining strength, Christians owe him a deep sense of gratefulness. Ingratitude lies at the heart of rebellion against God (Rom. 1:21). In arrogant pride people ignore God, choosing rather to credit themselves for the blessings of life. This ungrateful attitude has no place among believers. Thanksgiving is an attitude for all seasons. Hard times are as much an occasion for gratitude as good times (I Thess. 5:18). Even experiences that normally cause tension are to be faced with thankful prayer anticipating inward peace (Phil. 4:6,7). Knowing that God is in control and will use this hardship to promote spiritual growth is sufficient reason to pray thankfully (Rom. 8:28; James 1:2-4).

Intercession

Prayer is also a time to ask God to meet the needs of others. The phrase, "God first, others second, self last" applies well to prayer. Paul regularly prayed for the spiritual maturity of believers (Phil. 1:9-11; Eph. 1:16-23; 3:14-21) and asked them to pray for his consistent witness (Eph. 6:18-20). Through prayer you can contribute positively to the lives of others way beyond the limits of your personal resources and capacities (Phil. 1:19).

Requests

Finally, prayer is telling God all the details of everything that concerns you (Phil. 4:6). Seeking help from God for personal challenges, problems, and opportunities is not selfish. Jesus encouraged his disciples to take their requests to God in his name (John 16:23,24). Through prayer you receive divine help for daily needs.

■ Results of prayer in the Bible ■

Prayer played a vital part in the lives of God's people in biblical times. The Old Testament leaders Abraham, Moses, Nehemiah, and Ezra, godly Job, and Hannah, the prophets Samuel, Elijah, Elisha, Jonah, Daniel, and Jeremiah, and the kings David, Solomon, and Hezekiah all witnessed God's direct involvement in their lives through prayer. Although Jesus is God, during his life on earth he prayed regularly to his heavenly Father. Following his teaching, the apostles and later the early church, placed a priority on prayer. In all these cases, God followed no single pattern in responding to his people's requests. Whether the loving divine answer was "Yes," "Wait," or "No," prayer greatly affected their lives.

Granting of requests

The Old Testament contains many examples of how God grants requests.

Israel's early leaders knew the power of prayer. When Abraham prayed for Abimelech, king of Gerar, the king's life was spared and his family was able to have children again (Gen. 20:17,18). Several times during the wilderness wanderings Moses prayed for the rebellious Israelites and God spared them from threatened destruction (Num. 11:2; 14:12-16; 21:7).

The history of the nation Israel was one of recurring defection from God, divine discipline, and prayer-secured deliverance. After the people repented for their idolatry, God broke the Philistine dominance over them in answer to Samuel's prayer (I Sam. 7:5-13). Later, when Saul became Israel's first king, Samuel showed God's displeasure at their wanting a king like other nations by praying down a thunderstorm. In spite of Israel's sin, Samuel also prayed for their well-being (I Sam. 12:16-23).

When David and Solomon reigned over the united kingdom, Israel was led by men of prayer. Many Psalms are prayers of David (Psalm 17; 72:20; 86; 142). David's confession concerning his sin with Bathsheba is a pattern for all subsequent generations (Psalm 51). Solomon's prayer for wisdom at his coronation (I Kings 3:7-9) and humility in his prayer dedicating the temple brought divine blessing on the whole nation.

In the New Testament prayer continues its crucial role. During his earthly ministry, Jesus' prayers were directly connected with the descent of the Holy Spirit upon him at his baptism (Luke 3:21,22), times of heavy ministry (Mark 1:35; Luke 5:16), the selection of the disciples (Luke 6:12), the confession by Peter that he was "the Christ, the Son of the living God" (Luke 9:18-20; Matt. 16:16), his transfiguration on the mountain (Luke 9:29), and his betrayal and crucifixion (Luke 22:40-44). Through prayer the early church received guidance in the choice of an apostle to replace Judas (Acts 1:24), courage to witness during times of persecution (Acts 4:31), the initial outpouring of the Holy Spirit on Samaritan believers (Acts 8:15), God's orders to reach out to Gentiles (Acts 10:9-23), divine initiation and enablement for Paul's missionary journeys (Acts 13:1-3), the appointment of local church leaders (Acts 14:23), and release from prison (Acts 12:12; 16:25-40). Answering prayer, God guided, equipped, and enabled the early church for effective ministry.

Delaying until a better time

Even in biblical times God did not always answer his people's requests immediately. Sometimes God waited for his right time. The heavens seemed closed to the cries of Job as his family's circumstances went from bad to worse. But God's answer was not "No." By delaying the end of Job's suffering, God taught his servant valuable spiritual lessons which could only be learned in adversity. Ultimately Job emerged as a more mature child of God with restored health and doubled finances (Job 3:11-23; 7:20; 42:8-10; James 5:11). Married couples unable to have children waited and yearned and waited again, despairing of ever having a family. In God's perfect time Hannah conceived her son, Samuel (I Sam. 1:5-7, 20) and Elizabeth and Zechariah bore John the Baptist (Luke 1:13).

Affirming a superior way

At times the believer's wiser heavenly Father lovingly denies a request because he knows what is best for his begging child. Only a cruel parent would have granted Elijah's (I Kings 19:4) or Jonah's (Jonah 4:1-10) prayers for death. Being depressed, the prophets were not thinking clearly, so God said, "No." Death was no solution for prophets who had just been God's instruments for revival.

Often God denied a specific request not because it was foolish or bad, but because he had something better in mind. Paul's "thorn in the flesh" is an example of this. On three occasions Paul "pleaded with the Lord to take it away." God refused but assured Paul, "My grace is sufficient for you, for my power is made perfect in weakness" (II Cor. 12:7-10 NIV). Paul discovered that the spiritual blessing supplied by God's grace in times of adversity far surpassed any inconvenience or pain.

■ Results of prayer today ■

Prayer continues to be an effective force in the modern world. Although many non-Christians in this scientific age deny supernatural intervention in daily events, evidence abounds that God still answers prayer. The requests of God's people influence individual lives and international affairs today as much as they did in biblical times. One does not need to be a special superhuman Christian to realize the power of prayer. Elijah, that person who controlled the weather by his prayers, "was a man just like us" (James 5:17 NIV). Like many today, he was subject to times of discouragement and fear, yet God answered his prayers.

Definite answers to prayer

Testimonies abound to God's faithful answers to the requests of his children. Believers imprisoned for their faith report receiving courage and spiritual strength when they prayed. Some suffering from serious life-threatening illnesses have been miraculously healed because God's people prayed. The church has grown in nations where Christianity is illegal or suppressed in answer to the prayers of foreign believers not allowed in those countries. Lives wrecked by sin have been transformed by a conversion experience that has come after years of faithful prayer by a relative or close friend. Many rejoice in the multitude of daily needs that God specifically provides as they pray.

Realistic expectations in prayer

Believers often experience frustration when they do not see direct results from their prayers. Some accuse God of not keeping his word, when in reality they have misunderstood his promises concerning prayer. Jesus' promise that the Father would give "whatsoever" his disciples asked (John 16:23,24) must not be taken to mean that God will always do precisely what believers want. Prayer is a request to God for help, not a demand for action. This is a proverbial type promise that states a general truth without indicating any qualifications or exceptions. Other passages make it clear that requests motivated by selfish desire (James 4:3) or opposed to God's will are not answered (I John 5:14). Answers to prayer are not some kind of demand performance by God. He is not under any contractual obligation to give everything his people want. God evaluates every prayer by his infinite wisdom and unfailing love. He gives only what he knows is best.

Some believe that the answer is guaranteed when two people agree, failing to realize that this promise has to do with church discipline, not prayer for things (Matt. 18:19). This passage deals with reconciliation and forgiveness. The agreement concerns the kind of discipline that God should bring upon an unrepentant guilty party. It is dangerous to give false expectations based on misunderstanding Scripture. When prayers are not answered positively, people feel that God has failed them. They become disappointed in God for something he never promised to do.

Confident assurance in prayer

From limited human perspective, disease, hardships, adversity, and persecution seem totally negative. Given the option, Christians would veto having these experiences invade their lives. Yet, these problems are a part of the sinful, fallen world in which believers live out their Christian faith. God hates these terrible results of the fall and has acted decisively in Christ defeating Satan who has the power of death (Heb. 2:14). Knowing that God "is able to do exceeding abundantly above all that we ask or think according to the power that worketh in us," that same power which he used in Christ's resurrection and ascension (Eph. 3:20; 1:19-22), believers should pray for with confidence. Nothing is too hard for God.

God promises to come to the aid of his children in these hard circumstances, but never to exempt them from such difficulties. In fact, Jesus clearly warns his disciples that they will have tribulation in this world. He offers peace within these crises, not immunity from them (John 16:33). As in biblical times, God sometimes chooses to glorify his name by miraculously removing the problem, at other times, by strengthening believers so that they can persevere to God's glory. Anytime

God chooses not to heal sickness or remove a difficult problem, his children should rest in confident assurance that God will give some better spiritual benefit.

■ Summary ■

Prayer is an essential element in growing toward spiritual maturity. It is your means of one-to-one communication with God. The Bible provides numerous examples of all types of prayers and God's answers to them. They should be used as guides in your own prayer life. You should be concerned that your prayer life includes balanced elements of the following: worship, confession, adoration, praise, thanksgiving, intercession, and requests. Spiritual growth involves learning to accept God's answers to your prayers as his will. Prayer is a powerful force and it needs to be practiced continuously as you mature in your Christian life.

■ Discussion Questions ■

1. Name four things which prayer does not do and explain why.
2. Since prayer doesn't do these things, why pray?
3. Discuss how each of the seven aspects of a balanced prayer life aid spiritual growth.
4. Explain how prayer was involved in God's disciplining of his people in the Old Testament.
5. Why is it wrong to think that prayer guarantees you will get everything you request?
6. How can "wait" or "no" be viewed as positive answers to prayer?
7. Identify some false expectations which people have concerning prayer and discuss why these are a serious problem.

■ Application Activities ■

1. Keep a prayer journal recording all requests and answers. Divide each page into four vertical columns with the headings: Date, Prayer request, Answer, and Date answered.
2. In your personal Bible study, read Luke and Acts, one chapter per day, recording in a separate section of your prayer journal every reference to prayer. For each prayer write the occasion, subject matter, aspects of prayer, and answer if one is reported.
3. Study the great prayers in the Bible identifying the various aspects of prayer in each one.

■ Bibliography ■

Bounds, E. M. *Power Through Prayer*. Chicago: Moody Press, n.d.

Murray, Andrew. *With Christ in the School of Prayer*. Old Tappan, NJ: Revell, 1953.

Kelly, Thomas R. *A Testament of Devotion*. New York: Harper and Brothers Publishers, 1941.

GROWING
INWARDLY

ESTABLISHING A
GODLY LIFESTYLE

4 Christians wanting to grow spiritually will impact the world only to the degree they live what they say they believe. Holiness is not an option for the growing Christian. It is a prerequisite for service in the kingdom of God. A pure heart is required for servants of an holy God.

Yet God does not require moral perfection from his disciples. One only has to look at the heroes of the faith in Hebrews 11 to see that God uses men and women in spite of their moral imperfections and weaknesses. It was in their weakness that they were made strong (Heb. 11:34). The fact, however, that God uses weak and sinful people to accomplish his plans does not give believers an excuse to live in sin. Rather it should, as the author of Hebrews suggests, challenge them to get rid of the sin in their lives and press on in the race of faith (Heb. 12:1,2).

Holiness is not merely living up to some superficial human standard of perfection. Holiness is an attitude of the heart that expresses itself in godly living. In order to establish such an holy, godly lifestyle, you must first cultivate a heart for God; second, overcome temptations in your life; and third, establish patterns of holy living.

■ Cultivate a heart for God ■

Godliness is an attitude of the heart that radiates itself in godly behavior. Growing Christians must cultivate a heart for God in order to establish a godly lifestyle.

The word "heart" throughout Scripture portrays the whole inner life of persons including their minds, emotions, and wills. The Holy Spirit desires to fill their hearts with his supernatural presence. As the heart is filled up with God, it overflows into words, actions, and godly behavior. Godly lifestyle flows from hearts filled with the Spirit of God.

In order to cultivate a godly heart, you as a Christian wanting to continue to grow and mature in your faith must first, open your life to God; second, confess all known sin; and third, desire the fullness of the Holy Spirit.

Open up to God

God has never been satisfied with service and worship that is "put on" the way a person might put on a coat or hat. Such religious activity is futile unless it comes from the heart (Isa. 29:13). God has commanded that his people love him with their whole beings—heart, mind, soul, and might (Deut. 6:5; Matt. 22:37). In order to do so believers must allow the Spirit of God to penetrate every area of their inner lives.

In Jeremiah, God tells his people: "break up your fallow ground, and sow not among thorns. Circumcise yourselves to the Lord, and take away the foreskins of your heart" (Jer. 4:3,4).

The first part of this metaphor compares people's hearts to a hard, unkept field in which weeds have been allowed to grow. In the second part God commands his people to cut off the covering of their heart to allow his Word to change their lives. Disgusted with his people's sinful lifestyle, God commands them to cultivate and break up their hard hearts and allow the Spirit of God to change their sinful lives.

Likewise, if you are to continue to grow and mature as a Christian, you must allow the Spirit of God to break up hard areas in your heart. You must cultivate a tender heart for God.

Confess your sin to God

Once you, as a growing Christian, have opened up the secret and hidden places of your heart to God, you must confess specific sins before God (I John 1:9). The simple, humble confession of sin before God opens the door of forgiveness, healing, and power for the believer. The power of the almighty God is activated in humble hearts, sensitive to the conviction of the Holy Spirit (Isa. 57:15).

To continue to grow spiritually, you must develop the daily practice of examining your heart and your actions before God and confessing known sin.

Desire the fullness of the Holy Spirit

Once you have dealt ruthlessly with known sin, you should seek the fullness of the Holy Spirit. Being filled with the Holy Spirit empowers you for service. The Holy Spirit was given to the church in part to empower it to witness (Acts 1:8). Believers are commanded to continue to be filled with the Holy Spirit (Eph. 5:18).

Throughout the Old Testament, believers are compelled to seek God. As the psalmist states: "As the hart panteth after the water brooks, so panteth my soul after thee, O God. My soul thirsteth for God, for the living God" (Ps. 42:1,2).

What was experienced only periodically by people of God in the Old Testament, now is a permanent gift to the church in the New Testament. Jesus, in reference to the gift of the Holy Spirit, quotes Isaiah 44:3, "Out of his belly shall flow rivers of living water" (John 7:38).

As these and other Scriptures indicate, the Holy Spirit not only fills people's hearts but also flows out into the lives of others. Paul's prayer in Ephesians 3:14-21 serves as a model of how the Holy Spirit works in believers' hearts. Paul begins by asking believers to "be strengthened with might by his Spirit in the inner man" and ends with the prayer that they "might be filled with all the fulness of God." There is a tremendous power available for Christians through the Person of the Holy Spirit. By being filled with the Holy Spirit, believers receive power to witness, reflecting the fullness of God through their lifestyles.

Establishing a godly lifestyle begins with cultivating a heart for God. It demands discipline and perseverance in maintaining a daily time of reflection, Bible study, and prayer. By writing reflections, concerns, and prayers in a journal, you can keep yourself accountable to God for your personal growth.

■ Overcome temptation ■

You, as a growing Christian, are as susceptible to temptation as much as any believer. Just because you are being used by God doesn't mean you are sheltered from Satan's schemes. It may even mean that Satan will fight harder to bring you into temptation. If you are to have a godly lifestyle, you must learn how to overcome temptation in life.

There are three practical ways you can overcome temptation: first, admit your weaknesses; second, use God's resources; and third, guard your thought life.

Admit your weaknesses

Some believers, in an attempt to keep a good image in front of others, act as if they never struggle with sin or temptation. They often feel that if they share their struggles, they will come across as being weak. Yet Scripture reveals a different model of the "ideal Christian."

Going back to the heroes of faith mentioned in Hebrews, the biblical author states that these heroes "out of weakness were made strong" (Heb. 11:34). Paul specifically states that "strength is made perfect in weakness" (II Cor. 12:7-10). The power of the Holy Spirit seems to be activated in believers' lives when they are humbly aware of their own weaknesses.

When Christians get too confident and proud, they are more apt to depend on their own talents and abilities and leave God out. "Wherefore let him that thinketh he standeth take heed lest he fall" (I Cor. 10:12).

Scripture provides graphic illustrations of great leaders like Saul, David, and Solomon who fell into temptation, at least in part, because of pride. To grow spiritually you must be willing to admit your weaknesses, sins, struggles, and failures. You must keep a humble heart before God and other people. Jeremiah 17:9 states that "the heart is deceitful above all things." This statement applies not only to the heathen but also to believers. In order to overcome temptation, you must admit to yourself, God, and others your weaknesses and struggles.

Use God's resources

The psalmist makes a direct connection between his weakness and God's strength in Psalm 73:26: "My flesh and my heart faileth, but God is the strength of my heart, and my portion forever."

The power of God is unleashed when you humbly depend on him for strength in the midst of your human weakness. God's resources are available for you to overcome temptation. God promises you that as you draw near to him, he will draw closer to you. As you approach God with a humble heart, he promises to give you the resources you need to overcome temptation (James 4:7-10).

The key to overcoming temptation is to find strength in the Lord and his resources. In Ephesians 6:10-20, Paul refers to some of God's resources as the "armor of God." Defensively he challenges Christian soldiers to protect themselves with truth, righteousness, the message of the gospel of peace, faith, and salvation. Offensively he challenges believers to arm themselves with the Word of God and persistent prayer. While many of these resources at first glance seem to be theologically abstract, they have a great deal of practical value to believers.

You, as a growing, maturing Christian, need to use God's Word as a basis on which to identify Satan's deceptive schemes. Protected by the righteousness of God, through the atonement of Jesus Christ, you can ignore the false accusations of Satan. You can dispel feelings of aimlessness by continually following Christ's Great Commission. Armed with faith, you are enabled to overcome the momentary hurts and obstacles in life and press on in spite of disappointments. The fact of salvation protects you from the fear of falling away from the faith because of some failure or weakness.

Finally, you, as a growing Christian, should wield God's Word to silence the accusations of Satan and to shed light on the path ahead.

Through these resources God makes it possible for you to overcome temptation.

Guard your thought life
Sin comes from the heart (Matt. 15:18). Any strategy to overcome temptation must begin with the heart. If a sinful thought or desire is not dealt with immediately, it may lead to sinful behavior. When Christians fall, it usually is because they have allowed sinful thoughts and desires to burn unrestrained in their hearts over a period of time. The way to overcome such temptations is to learn to discipline thoughts.

Paul, in his explanation of how he avoided falling into Satan's schemes, states that believers are "bringing into captivity every thought to the obedience of Christ" (II Cor. 10:5). If you are to continue to grow and mature in Christ, you must guard your heart from any thought or desire that would violate scriptural principles or laws.

By dealing ruthlessly with sin at the thought level, you are more apt to refrain from sinful actions. At the first indication of a tempting thought, quote an appropriate Scripture verse or softly sing a hymn. By drawing your thoughts to God, you will receive deliverance from temptation.

■ Establishing patterns of holy living ■
To continue to grow as a Christian, your lifestyle must be consistent with biblical principles of holiness. While establishing a godly lifestyle

begins in the heart, its evidence is seen in daily behavior. Godly actions and deeds spring from a pure heart and disciplined lifestyle. In order to establish patterns of holy living, you must first maintain biblical standards; second, discipline all areas of your life; and third, be accountable to other Christians.

Maintain biblical standards

God commands Christians to be holy and blameless in their behavior simply because of the fact that he is holy (I Pet. 1:15; Lev. 11:44). If you are to be Christlike, then you must strive to be like him in holiness.

The standard of holiness must be God's standard, perfect holiness. Rather than adopt the standards of morality practiced in the world or even in the church, you, as a growing Christian, must continually seek to live up to God's standards of holiness found in his Word.

The fact that believers will always fall short of God's perfect standard should not discourage them but rather drive them to the cross. Through Christ's blood sacrifice, he has completely justified believers (Rom. 5:8,9). There is no need for Christians to feel condemned for falling short of God's standard of holiness (Rom. 8:1). Through the blood of Christ, believers are made holy by an act of God (Gal. 3:2,3). As they walk in the light of the Word of God, the blood of Jesus cleanses them from all sin (I John 1:7).

You, as a growing Christian, must strive to live up to biblical standards of holiness not in order to earn God's favor or to appease his wrath but rather as a heartfelt response to his mercy and grace. The challenge Paul gives Christians in Romans 12:1,2 makes this clear: "I beseech you therefore brethren, by the mercies of God, that ye present your bodies a living sacrifice, holy, acceptable unto God, which is your reasonable service. And be not conformed to this world: but be ye transformed by the renewing of your mind, that ye may prove what is that good, and acceptable, and perfect, will of God."

It is amazing to think that by merely presenting your body to God as a living and holy sacrifice, you are "acceptable to God."

The secret to holy living is not perfection but the total commitment of your whole self to serve God. Rather than conforming to the standards and lifestyle of the world, you must live according to biblical standards of behavior. Your mind must reflect the thoughts and desires of the mind of Christ. As you allow your lifestyle to be transformed by the mind of Christ, you will become a living example of God's will—"good and acceptable and perfect." Patterns of holy living will be evidence of such a transformed heart and mind.

Discipline all areas of your life

Patterns of holy living do not come without hard work and discipline. Although Peter states that "his divine power hath given unto us all things that pertain unto life and godliness," his gift does not deny human responsibility. Throughout this passage Peter exhorts believers to "give diligence" and to "do these things." The passage as a whole seems to indicate that if people have truly become partakers of the divine nature of God, they will strive to grow in holiness (II Pet. 1:2-11). Paul also exhorts believers to discipline themselves for the purpose of godliness (I Tim. 4:7,8). Discipline involves hard work. It is not always enjoyable. In fact, most discipline is very difficult. Yet discipline is absolutely necessary in order to establish patterns of holy living (Heb. 12:1-11).

To grow spiritually, you must be disciplined in every area of life: social, mental, emotional, physical, and moral. Concerning your social life, you need to carefully evaluate the type of people you spend time with and the quality of your relationships. You also need to set goals for yourself concerning your intellectual development. This could mean setting up a regular pattern of stimulating reading, enrolling in a continuing education class, or attending a seminar or workshop. You must also guard your emotional life so that neither past concerns nor present pressures monopolize your time or energy. You must find healthy ways to express emotions through wholesome friendships, recreation, and hobbies. Keeping in shape physically through a regular exercise program and a healthy diet has a tremendous effect on both emotional and spiritual health.

Finally, you, as a growing Christian, need to maintain strict discipline in the moral and ethical areas of your life. Sexuality, power, and money all pose serious moral temptations to Christians in ministry and must be disciplined according to God's Word. Socially, mentally, emotionally, physically, and morally, you must maintain strict discipline in order to maintain a godly lifestyle.

Thus, the most important discipline in your life will be the daily study of God's Word. In a daily quiet time you must regularly and systematically study Scripture in order to understand and apply it to life. A daily time of prayer and personal reflection helps you to keep in tune with God. Regular fellowship and worship with a body of believers is another mandatory discipline for your growth in holy living. Without discipline in these areas, you may focus too much time on outward ministry-related activities while neglecting your heart. The result is often a shallow, busy ministry with little evidence of godliness.

Be accountable to godly Christians

Active Christians tend to be lone rangers. They often get going so fast and in so many directions that they fail to nurture quality relationships with other godly Christians to whom they can be held accountable. They may ignore character weaknesses hoping that God will overlook them. By the time some of these individuals seek help, it is too late. Their ministries, families, and relationships may have been severly hurt.

You, as a growing, maturing believer, need to make yourself accountable on a deep interpersonal level to at least one other godly Christian outside your immediate family. These individuals should be people with whom you can confess even the most personal sins and faults (James 5:16) and who should be able to encourage you in holy living and stay with you as you struggle in your "striving against sin" (Heb. 12:4).

It is a good practice for all believers to meet on a regular basis with such individuals or small group of godly believers. This practice keeps maturing Christians humble and insures growth towards godly lifestyles.

■ Summary ■

Your effectiveness in ministry depends on your ability to live a godly lifestyle. Godliness reproduces itself. In order to establish a godly lifestyle, you must first cultivate a heart for God by opening yourself up to God, confessing known sin, and allowing God to fill you with the power of the Holy Spirit. Second, you must learn to overcome temptation by admitting your weaknesses, using God's resources, and guarding your thought life. Third, you must establish patterns of holy living by maintaining biblical standards in your lifestyle, disciplining all areas of your life, and being accountable to other godly Christians.

■ Discussion Questions ■

1. What are the three steps to establishing a godly lifestyle?
2. What is the importance of daily confession of sin?
3. What part does the Holy Spirit play in establishing a godly lifestyle?
4. How can you overcome temptation?
5. Why is the guarding of your thought life important?
6. Why are biblical standards still "the" standards to live by?
7. Why is it important to be accountable to other Christians?

■ Application Activity ■

To best apply all the principles in this chapter, earnestly try to answer or identify the following as it pertains to your life.

1. What areas of your life have you tried to hide from God?
2. Ask God to forgive you for specific sins in your life.
3. Ask the Spirit of God to fill those areas of your heart where old desires and thoughts used to dwell.
4. List the areas of temptation that you struggle with.
5. How are you going to discipline your thought life?
6. How do your standards of behavior fall short of biblical standards?
7. In what areas of your life do you need more discipline?
8. Who are you going to become accountable to in order to grow in holiness?

■ Bibliography ■

Bridges, Jerry. *The Pursuit of Holiness.* Colorado Springs, CO: Navpress, 1978.

Brown, Colin, Editor. *Dictionary of New Testament Theology* Grand Rapids, MI: Zondervan Publishing House, 1976.

Foster, Richard. *Celebration of Discipline.* San Francisco, CA: Harper & Row Publishers, 1978.

DEVELOPING INTERPERSONAL SKILLS IN RELATIONSHIPS

Success in ministry for Christians who are growing toward spiritual maturity depends to a great extent on their ability to relate positively to other people. The Bible relates that growing Christians need to develop relationships within the family, the church, and the world.

■ A biblical basis ■

The Bible provides a solid theological rationale for Christians to develop positive relationships with other people. Three theological reasons include: first, the nature of fellowship; second, the nature of the church; and third, the command of Christ.

The nature of fellowship

The word "fellowship" comes from the Greek word "koinonia" literally meaning a sharing together, participation, or common ownership. When it is used within the context of the gathering of believers, it refers to the intimate relationship that believers have with Jesus Christ and to one another. These two relationships are closely linked together in Scripture. John states that "which we have seen and heard declare we unto you, that ye also may have fellowship with us: and truly our fellowship is with the Father, and with His Son Jesus Christ"(I John 1:3).

This close connection between the believer's relationship with God and his/her relationship with other believers is seen again a few verses later: "If we say that we have fellowship with him, and walk in darkness, we lie, and do not the truth: but if we walk in the light as he is in the light, we have fellowship one with another, and the blood of Jesus Christ his Son cleanseth us from all sin" (I John 1:6,7).

This organic connection between the believer's relationship with Jesus Christ and his/her relationship with other people is seen clearly in Scripture: "Beloved, if God so loved us, we ought also to love one another. No man hath seen God at any time. If we love one another, God dwelleth in us, and his love is perfected in us" (I John 4:11,12).

The fellowship of the saints is a supernatural union of believers with one another around their common master, the Lord Jesus Christ. The biblical concept of "fellowship" demands that Christians care deeply for one another out of their common loyalty to Jesus Christ (I Cor. 10:16; Heb. 13:16; Rom. 15:2,6; Phil. 2:1).

The nature of the church

The church by definition is a body of believers joined together by their common commitment to Jesus Christ. As a body, the church is held together by the proper relationships of its members to one another. Paul wrote to the Ephesians concerning this, "The whole body, being fitted and held together by that which every joint supplies, according to the proper working of each individual part causes the growth of the body for the building up of itself in love" (Eph. 4:16 NASB).

The growth of the body of Christ depends upon how well all members use their gifts and talents to serve and build up other people.

The Bible uses many other models to represent the nature of the church—household, flock, kingdom, family, and community. Each model holds together because of close relationships between members and their Lord. Strong relationships within the church are like mortar holding a building together.

The command of Christ

Christians should work diligently at developing loving relationships with other people simply because Jesus commands it: "A new commandment I give unto you, that ye love one another; as I have loved you, that ye also love one another" (John 13:34).

Jesus not only commanded his followers to love one another, he showed them how to do it. Earlier in John 13, John records Jesus washing the feet of his disciples. Following this act of love, Jesus says, "If I then, your Lord and Master, have washed your feet; ye also ought to wash one another's feet. For I have given you an example, that ye should do as I have done to you" (John 13:14,15).

When Jesus told his disciples to love others as he had loved them, they knew exactly what he was saying. He had spent the last years of his life modeling in very concrete ways what love was all about. He had invested his life into their lives in ways they would never forget.

■ Developing relationships within the family ■

The family is the laboratory in which people learn to relate to one another. The interpersonal skills and behaviors learned in the home are carried over into other areas of a person's life. Good family relationships are basic to developing relationships within the church and world.

Husbands and wives

Psychologists and educators alike generally agree that one of the most significant indicators of a healthy family is a good relationship between husband and wife. It is not surprising that when the Bible deals with family life issues, it begins with the relationships between husbands and wives. In both Ephesians and Colossians Paul begins his teaching on the family with instructions to husbands and wives.

Paul in Ephesians precedes his advice to husbands and wives with a general statement to all believers: "submitting yourselves one to another in the fear of God" (Eph. 5:21). The forthcoming advice to husbands and wives must be understood in light of this command to both men and women. Because of a common reverence for God, believers, regardless of gender, are to esteem others higher than themselves.

With this principle in practice, husbands and wives can quite easily fulfill their roles suggested by Paul within the family. Wives are instructed to be subject to their husbands and husbands are told to love their wives. Without debating the various positions relating to the changing roles of men and women in families today, it seems as if Paul is putting as much responsibility on the husband as he is the wife for developing loving relationships within the home. While the wife is challenged to submit to and respect her husband, the husband is commanded to love his wife as Christ loves the church (Eph. 5:22-33). It is interesting that both of these commands are given in other passages of Scripture to believers without regard to gender.

If you are married, it is essential that you work diligently to develop submissive and loving relationships with your spouse. Such relationships model the organic relationship between Jesus Christ and his church. Couples need to plan mutually enjoyable activities with each other—regular Friday night dates, occasional mini-vacations for two, quiet evenings at home, regular times of prayer, and occasional rendezvous for lunch. Special times like these are essential in building warmth and trust in relationships between you and your husband or wife.

Parents and children

The temptation for many Christians is to get so involved in ministry that they neglect their children. In the case of younger Christians, still living with their parents, their tendency may be to draw away from their parents the more they get involved in ministry. Christians need to be challenged to be more sensitive to the needs of their children and parents. Relationships take time to build. Children need to have plenty of time to spend with their parents if they are to assimilate the biblical values that the parents hold. The quality of the relationship between parent and child often determines whether or not the child follows the biblical values held by the parents.

Growing Christians must invest whatever time is necessary to develop quality relationships with their family members.

■ Developing relationships within the church ■

Growth within the church is dependent upon the quality of the relationships between believers. Believers are challenged in Scripture to edify, confess faults, empathize, submit to, and accept one another.

Edify one another
The Bible uses the term "edify" to signify the process of building up and strengthening one another in the body of Christ (Eph. 4:16). Believers build up one another primarily by encouraging one another (Rom. 14:19; I Thess. 5:11).

This skill is particularly important for you to develop if you wish to become active in ministry since the volunteers you may work with are seldom motivated by outward rewards. Research with church volunteers indicates that the primary skill needed to motivate others in ministry is the ability to support and encourage. Secular research also reaffirms the need for leaders to praise and affirm their workers. Christians can build up one another with words of encouragement, notes of appreciation, fresh baked cookies, and other deeds of kindness. Simple tokens of encouragement like flowers or cards often say much more than words.

Confess faults to one another
You, like all Christians, are bound to make mistakes. Whether it is forgetting an announcement, missing an appointment, or hurting someone's feelings, you are bound to make occasional blunders. Even in your personal life, sins and mistakes are bound to happen.

The sign of growing Christians is their ability to confess sin and weakness. By readily acknowledging their weaknesses and mistakes, they show others that they are teachable and humble.

Confessing faults before God and others keeps you accountable to the body of Christ (James 5:16).

Empathize with one another
Paul challenges the Christian to: "regard one another as more important than himself; do not merely look out for your own personal interests, but also for the interest of others" (Phil. 2:3,4 NASB).

Growing Christians must see things from the perspective of the people they are working with. They need to identify with the feelings of other people. In sorrow, growing Christians need to bear the emotional burdens of other believers (Gal. 6:2). In the midst of another believer's joy, they need to celebrate (Rom. 12:15).

Submit to one another
Mutual submission is not a suggestion, it is a command (Eph. 5:21). It implies that believers should regard themselves as being under the authority of other Christians, being sensitive to their needs and wishes. It mandates that Christians listen to the ideas of others. Believers are commanded to submit to the governing authorities (Rom. 13:1; Titus 3:1; I Pet. 2:13), spiritual leaders (I Cor. 16:16), and elders (I Pet. 5:5).

If you desire to continue to grow and mature in Christ, you need to develop an attitude of humble respect for the people in leadership positions to whom you are responsible.

Accept one another

The church of Jesus Christ combines men, women, and children from various cultures, nationalities, traditions, languages, and political persuasions. There are bound to be tensions and barriers based upon these differences. Yet, in spite of these differences, the church by nature is a unified body. The church will live out this theological distinctive only as members accept one another.

You, as a growing, maturing Christian, must avoid the temptation to work only with those with whom you agree. You must go out of your way to develop closer relationships with people from various social, economic, and political backgrounds.

■ Developing relationships within the world ■

One of the tests of Christian people's spirituality is their ability to relate to people in the world. If the church is going to fulfill the Great Commission, it must infiltrate the world by developing close relationships with non-Christians. Yet in drawing close to people who have opposing values and lifestyles, Christians must be careful not to become squeezed into a worldly value system.

Jesus' example in the world

The Pharisees criticized Jesus for befriending tax-gatherers and sinners (Luke 7:34). In fact, Jesus himself said that his mission was not to the so-called "righteous" but to the sinners (Matt. 9:13). Jesus spent a great deal of his time building relationships with people who were considered the worst of sinners. Yet he was able to develop relationships with sinners without being affected by their ungodly values.

You, too, need to follow this example. Don't get so wrapped up in committees, projects, programs, and meetings with church people that you have no time or energy left to develop close relationships with non-Christians. You must maintain a balance in your personal relationships between Christians and non-Christians.

Friendship evangelism

God uses many evangelistic approaches to draw people into his kingdom. Friendship evangelism is an approach simply based upon building relationships with non-Christians in normal daily contacts. Within such relationships Christians look for opportunities to demonstrate love and to share their faith. Obviously, the success of such an approach depends to a great extent upon people's ability to develop caring relationships with other people.

You, as a growing and maturing Christian, must be able to ask appropriate questions, listen, empathize, and tactfully bring in the gospel message at the right time. You must be able to maintain friendships with non-Christians in spite of their apparent apathy towards spiritual things. If you are going to be effective at friendship evangelism, you must put a high priority on building personal relationships.

In your attempt to develop close interpersonal relationships with non-Christians, you must be cautious not to compromise your biblical values and standards.

James 4:4 warns the Christian that "friendship of the world is enmity with God." Here James makes a distinction between friendship with "worldly people" and friendship with "worldly values." While Christians are commanded to develop loving relationships with people in the world, they are warned not to allow worldly values to influence them.

You must be very careful not to sacrifice biblical principles and values in an attempt to relate to non-Christians.

■ Dealing with problems ■

Where there are people, there are problems. The church is no different than other organizations in this regard. As you seek to grow spiritually, you must prepare yourself to deal with problems in relationships. Many times, however, apparent problems between Christians turn out to be catalysts for growth when handled properly. In order to deal redemptively with problems and interpersonal conflicts, you must learn to forbear, admonish, and forgive.

Forbear one another

Christians are not perfect people. They have personality weaknesses, bad habits, annoying mannerisms, and personal struggles.

If you, as a growing, maturing Christian, are to have a positive influence on other people, you must learn to bear patiently with offensive people.

Paul challenges believers in these words: "walk worthy of the vocation wherewith ye are called, with all lowliness and meekness, with longsuffering, forbearing one another in love; endeavoring to keep the unity of the Spirit in the bond of peace" (Eph. 4:1-3).

Just as God shows patient forbearance with mankind, Christians must patiently "put up with" many of the offensive behaviors of other Christians. In the process of maturing, most sincere Christians will gradually "put off" behaviors that are offensive and "put on" those more consistent with the fruits of the Spirit.

As you mature as a Christian, you must be careful not to take upon yourself the total task of "perfecting the saints." Your first response to another Christian who may "rub you the wrong way" should be one of patient forbearance.

Admonish one another

There are situations, however, in which Christians must admonish other believers. When Christian friends are becoming increasingly involved in sin that is seriously affecting their Christian growth, fellow Christians are encouraged to admonish the other persons.

Paul admonishes individuals in the Corinthian church for their obvious immorality (I Cor. 4:14). In speaking to the church in Ephesus, which was being confronted with false teachers, Paul says: "Therefore be on the alert, remembering that night and day for a period of three years I did not cease to admonish each one with tears" (Acts 20:31 NASB).

Admonishing involves tactfully telling other persons how their attitudes or behaviors violate God's Word and retards their spiritual growth. To be most effective, everyone needs to have good relationships before the encounter. If hostility exists, the admonition is seldom accepted.

It is imperative for you, as a growing Christian, to develop trust and respect in your relationships before attempting to admonish other persons. Respect is earned through patient forbearance with another person.

Forgive one another

If you are to be effective in ministry, you must never allow bitterness or resentment to enter your heart.

Paul writes: "Let all bitterness, and wrath, and anger, and clamour, and evil speaking, be put away from you, with all malice: And be ye kind one to another, tenderhearted, forgiving one another, even as God for Christ's sake hath forgiven you" (Eph. 4:31,32).

Inevitably, you will be hurt or offended by someone during the course of your ministry. This cannot be avoided when working with people. Yet you must be very careful how you deal with your hurt feelings. If they are not handled properly, they can destroy your ministry.

As mentioned earlier, some offensive behavior of others should be merely ignored and forgotten. Other behavior needs to be tactfully confronted. If people sincerely ask for forgiveness, the problem usually resolves itself. If, however, people refuse to accept the responsibility for their sins or perhaps blame other persons, the problem will usually intensify. At this point, in which the individual has become "hardened in his heart," you may be tempted to hold bitter feelings. The appropriate response, however, must be to forgive the person.

When Peter asked Jesus how many times he should forgive a person who offended him, Jesus responded, "I do not say unto thee, until seven times: but until seventy times seven" (Matt. 18:22).

As a growing and maturing Christian, you must be willing to forgive any person who hurts you, no matter what the situation. Bitterness must never be allowed to take root in your heart.

■ Summary ■

Success in ministry depends a great deal upon your ability to relate to other people. Biblically, there are three theological reasons why developing interpersonal skills in relationships is important: first, the nature of "fellowship" mandates sharing; second, the nature of the "church" as the body of Christ implies interpersonal communication; and third, Jesus Christ commands Christians to love one another.

You, as a growing Christian, are responsible to develop skills in relating to your family, your church, and the world. You need to spend priority time with your spouse and children. In your relationships with people in the church, you need to develop skills in edifying, confessing faults, empathizing, submitting, and accepting others. In your relationship to people in the world, you need to follow Jesus' example by aggressively developing friendships with non-Christians while being careful not to assimilate their non-Christian values. Finally, you need to develop the ability to deal redemptively with problems in relationships by learning to forbear, admonish, and forgive.

■ Discussion Questions ■

1. List the three biblical reasons why Christians should develop positive relationships.
2. Why are family relationships important to the maturing Christian?
3. What are the five elements upon which Christians should rely in building relationships within the church?
4. Why is edification important to ministry?
5. Why is submission important to spiritual growth?
6. What is the major challenge to the Christian in developing relationships with non-Christians?
7. What three concepts need to be used when dealing with problem areas between Christians?

■ Application Activity ■

To best apply the principles presented in this chapter ask yourself these questions.

1. Why is it important for you to develop your interpersonal skills?
2. What are your strongest interpersonal skills?
3. What are your weakest interpersonal skills?
4. If married, what are some things you can do to improve your relationship with your spouse?
5. If you have children, what are some things you can do to improve your relationship with each of your children?
6. If you are a young adult, how can you improve your relationship with your parents?
7. Why is it difficult for you to submit to some people?
8. What kind of people do you find it difficult to accept?
9. How can you improve or develop your relationships with non-Christians?

■ Bibliography ■

Hartville, Sue. *Reciprocal Living*. Coral Gables, FL: West Indies Mission, 1976.

Pippert, Rebecca Manley. *Out of the Salt Shaker and into the World*. Downers Grove, IL: InterVarsity Press, 1979.

White, Jerry and Mary. *Friends and Friendships: The Secrets of Drawing Closer*. Colorado Springs, CO: NavPress, 1982.

CREATING A
SATISFYING
WORSHIP AND
DEVOTIONAL LIFE

Christians who are growing toward spiritual maturity are developing new relationships with their fellow believers. They also have a new relationship with God, their heavenly Father, and with Jesus Christ, their Lord. An experiential knowledge of God (Luke 10:21,22; John 14:7; Gal. 4:9) has replaced their former ignorance of God (Acts 17:30; I Cor. 15:34; Eph. 4:18). Where there was once enmity (Rom. 5:10) and hatred toward God (John 15:23; Rom. 1:30), there is now reconciliation (II Cor. 5:10; Rom. 5:11; Col. 1:21,22), friendship (John 15:13-15), love (I John 4:19-21), and even worship (John 4:23,24; Phil. 3:3). Surely Christians have progressed a long way (Luke 15:13,20; Eph. 2:13,17) from where they were as unbelievers.

■ What is worship ■
Worship comes from the Anglo-Saxon *weorthscipe* which meant "to ascribe worth, to pay homage, to reverence or venerate." It was modified to *worthship* and then finally to *worship*. It refers to worth or worthiness. People worship that which is worthy. People and idols are not worthy of worship; only God is worthy of this. "Thou art worthy, O Lord, to receive glory and honour and power" (Rev. 4:11). "Worthy is the Lamb that was slain" (Rev. 5:12). What people worship is a good indication of what is really valuable to them.

How can you bring worthy worship to the Most Worthy One? A helpful insight is found by considering how worship is done in heaven. In Rev. 4:10,11, the twenty-four elders around the throne of God prostrate themselves before the royal ruler on the throne. They, in their finiteness, worship the eternal one and give up their own glory (crowns) to him. They declare his worthship ("Thou art worthy") because he was the creator of all things. This is the central thought in worship.

Because of who God is and what he does, you should attribute to him the glory that is due his name (Ps. 95:1-7; 96:1-9; Rev. 5:12,13).

The essence of worship, then, is the celebration of God. It is not casual or careless but as thoughtful as you might put into celebrating a birthday or anniversary. It is not gifts given grudgingly or out of compulsion, but with hilarity (II Cor. 9:7). It is not haphazard music poorly done, nor merely performed, but offered with joy and spirit as Psalm 100 urges. It is an active response to God whereby you are not a passive spectator but a participant. It is not something you watch or that is done for you, but something you do.

■ Basics of worship ■

"Worship" translates four different Hebrew words in the King James Version, but the one used most often means "to bow down, to do homage." It was first used in Genesis 18:2 when Abraham bowed down to the three visitors, one of whom was the Lord.

Of the three Greek words used in the New Testament, the key word literally means "to kiss toward" (as kissing the earth to honor the deities of the earth). It conveys the idea of doing obeisance to God (John 4:21-24). In the gospels it is used of Jesus who is revered and worshiped as Messiah (Matt. 2:2,8,11; 14:33; 28:9,17).

True worship is an inner act of the spirit. External expression is neither a prerequisite nor a guarantee of worship. This is supported by the fact that in Acts the word translated *worship* is never used for Christian worship apart from the earliest worship in the temple.

Another important Greek word translated *worship* basically means "to serve, minister" (see Heb. 9:9,14; Rev. 22:3). It rests on a profound commitment to God in love and fear with no thought of reward and is far more comprehensive than that of being a slave.

Worship, in this sense, is a self-offering to God on the basis of his self-offering to you. God wants your entire being, and as you present it to him for use in his service, then all of life becomes a worship experience that goes beyond just one hour on Sunday morning. You can offer to God a service of worship in the way you perform your work, teach a Sunday school class, sing a solo, serve on a church board or committee, or give of your money. It can revolutionize your whole concept of Christian service if you begin to think of all ministry involvement as an act of worship, whether it be behind the scenes or in public.

When you consider all the words used for worship in the Bible, you discover that worship involves both attitudes (awe, reverence, respect) and actions (bowing, praising, serving). True worship is not a formality. It involves the mind, emotions, and the will. It must be intellectual, motivated by love, and lead to obedience of God's will (Rom. 12:1,2). The examples already given show that worship is both corporate and individual, public or private service for the Lord which is motivated by a reverence for him who is totally worthy.

Jesus revealed several basics about worship when he declared that it must be in spirit and in truth (John 4:23-26):

1. Worship can take place anywhere and everywhere since spirit is not confined to a particular place or time.
2. Worship is a person-to-person experience, honoring with your spirit God who was revealed through Jesus Christ.
3. Worship is subjective, spirited, involving the emotions as much as people do at weddings, funerals, and athletic events.
4. Worship must be genuine and without pretense. God hates insincere worship (Isa. 1:10-17; Mal. 1:7-14; Matt. 15:8,9). False worship is that which is not in accord with the revealed Word of God. Therefore, worshiping in truth necessitates a growing knowledge of the Word which will also increase believers' appreciation for the worth of the God they worship.
5. There is to be a balance between subjective experience and maintaining the objective truth of orthodoxy. Christians of various backgrounds and communions can express their worship in different ways that reflect their individual personalities and cultures, based on truth that never changes.
6. God seeks worshipers to worship him in this way.

Worship, then, is your response of all that God is and says and does. You are not to worship God for what you derive from worship, but because he is worthy.

■ Requirements for worship ■

All persons have the potential for worship (Phil. 2:10,11) but there are critical requirements for producing worship that God accepts.

First and foremost is the new birth. "No man can say that Jesus is the Lord, but by the Holy Ghost" (I Cor. 12:3). It is by the Holy Spirit that believers know who Christ is, that they love and adore him with the esteem of which he is worthy.

But not all Christians are able to worship because they are defiled by daily sin. The disciples learned that they needed their spiritual feet washed even though they had been spiritually bathed (John 13:2-15).

■ Priority of worship in the local church ■

A. W. Tozer once said that "Worship was the missing jewel of the church." Why is this?

Worship seems to be the weakest area of evangelical Christianity. The church is strongest in the areas of evangelism, teaching, and fellowship and there is a growing emphasis in applying the gospel to social and ethical concerns and in counseling. But depth of worship, where Christians sense the awesome presence and majesty of God, is seriously lacking in many churches.

Churches with pastors who excel in Bible teaching can minimize worship, for people can become spectators rather than participants. What is needed is a balance between a solid message from the Scriptures and a time of music, prayer, and quietness that exalts the glory and worth of the living

God; where, as Wesley expressed it, believers are "lost in wonder, love, and praise."

There have always been objections to this kind of worship. When Mary of Bethany poured her flask of oil over the head and feet of Jesus, some objected that this expense might better have been spent on the poor (Mark 14:4,5). As important as compassion for the poor is, a paraphrase of how Jesus responded to this act might be, "Let her alone, I like what she's doing. After I am gone you'll have plenty of time for social action" (Mark 14:6,7). Jesus put a priority on worship over service and declares it to be an important element of the gospel message (Mark 14:9).

There can be no substitute for being occupied with the majesty and splendor of God. You often hear the phrase "saved to serve." While service is a result of salvation, it is not the primary reason. God has saved you that you might magnify and extol his person. One way to do this is through service, but service to God is only one form of worship. Service is not only rendered by a bondslave, as Paul calls himself, but also a priest. Worship includes priestly service, but not all service includes worship. The teaching that believers are saved to serve (first and foremost) is so often advocated today that they can become over-engaged in religious activity. They think that God's plan for them is to be busy in the church, because the church is the best cause in the world in which to be involved. But this kind of activity leaves little time or energy for reflective worship.

Some advocate missions as the key to a spiritual church but it, like evangelism, must be a product of worship. Abraham, the first foreign missionary in the Bible, was told to leave his home and go to a distant land and there to bear witness for the true and living God. "The God of glory appeared unto our father Abraham" (Acts 7:2). This sounds a good deal like the experience of Isaiah who became an evangelist after worshiping in the temple and seeing God "high and lifted up" (Isa. 6:1). When missions come from a worship experience, the divine glory is emphasized as well as human need. Divorced from true worship, evangelism can become merely a program attached to an already over-loaded ecclesiastical machine.

On seeing the risen Lord in Galilee, the disciples worshiped him. It was to these adoring men that the Lord gave the Great Commission to go out and disciple all nations (Matt. 28:16-20). Paul's missionary call came to him while he was sharing in worship in the church at Antioch "as they ministered to the Lord, and fasted" (Acts 13:2).

■ The content of corporate worship ■

While the New Testament says little about the form and content of worship in the local church, there are some indications given in Acts 2, Acts 20, and I Corinthians 12-14.

The Word

The Old Testament Scriptures were held in high regard and thus were publicly read (I Tim. 4:13), along with Paul's epistles (I Thess. 5:27).

The Word was also preached to win converts and to build up believers (Acts 2:41; 4:2).

The Lord's Supper

Celebrating the Lord's Supper was a primary part of weekly worship. Acts 20:7 records a meeting on the first day of the week at which the disciples broke bread and Paul preached.

Prayer

Prayer was practiced both corporately and individually (Acts 2:42; 4:24; 6:4; 10:9; I Tim. 2:1-4). This included confession of sin, praise, petitions, intercession, and thanksgiving on behalf of all men.

Music

Worship may be possible without song, but nothing contributes more to its beauty and majesty than music. The Bible is full of the music of worship from Genesis to Relevation, but it is from David that believers learn the most about music in worship. He organized and provided for the support of skilled instrumentalists and choirs (I Chron. 25:1-6) to enhance Israel's worship.

The New Testament exhorts both private and public singing as a facet of worship. When believers are happy they should sing (James 5:13). Paul and Silas sang hymns of praise in jail (Acts 16:25). In Ephesians 5:19 and Colossians 3:16, psalms may reasonably refer to Old Testament psalms, perhaps with Christian additions, since many of the early believers were Jewish.

Hymns may be praises and testimonies directed to God and spiritual songs may include a wider variety of themes inspired by the Holy Spirit. Several New Testament passages may contain parts of early hymns (Eph. 5:14; I Tim. 3:16). Many doxologies which were spoken without musical accompaniment probably reflect early creedal statements (Rom. 11:33-36; 16:27; I Tim. 6:16).

Because of the importance of music in worship, singing should be encouraged for use by individuals privately, by groups, as solos, with or without instruments.

Giving

The New Testament says more about giving than any other single aspect of church life. The reference to a weekly allocation in I Corinthians 16:2, the liturgical significance given to a financial gift to Paul (Phil. 4:10-18), and mention of an offering in patristic writings have led to the view that an offering was a basic element in Christian worship. Liberality was taught as part of serving God (II Cor. 8:12; I Tim. 5:17,18).

Giving to others serves as clear proof of believers' love for God (James 2:15-17; I John 3:17,18). It should stem from a life that has first been given to them (II Cor. 8:5), should be voluntary (II Cor. 8:11,12; 9:7), cheerfully (I Cor. 9:7), and according to the measure of propriety that God gives them (I Cor. 16:2).

Other elements of worship may have included a confession of faith (I Tim. 6:12), a congregational "Amen" (I Cor. 14:16), and uplifted hands (I Tim. 2:8).

The above elements seemed to characterize the worship services of the early New Testament church. While not rigidly prescribed, they allow for creativity, flexibility, and adaptation to the local culture.

Should worship services be planned or spontaneous? Many have disagreed about this. In some fellowships, worship is spontaneous, led of the Spirit. To them, planned liturgy is unacceptable. Some churches are based on the practice of not being bound to any earthly authority that would dictate the form of worship. In other communions, worship follows a stated service or is planned by pastors and staff, sometimes with no design for immediate spontaneity. In either case, there should always be the leading of the Spirit.

■ Personal individual worship ■

Some pastors emphasize worship in their churches. Yet they find it difficult to lead a group of people in something that is not a part of their personal experience. In his book, *Growing Deep in the Christian Life,* Charles Swindoll tells of having to cultivate a *private* worship without talking about it, without spelling it out, or even confessing to the struggles of it. He added to his discipline of prayer such things as times of singing and quiet moments of silence. These times before the Lord were so delicate and elusive that he had to work out a way to fit them into his pressured schedule.

Worship should begin in your own personal devotional life. Start each day with God. Spend time meditating over the Word itself in Adoration, Confession, Thanksgiving, and Supplication (ACTS). As you begin with your own personal worship of God, you will grow to where this can spill over and touch the worship pattern of those around you in the church. Do not concentrate on cosmetic changes such as singing different hymns or rearranging the order of the service, but seek to produce an inner work of the Spirit in others' hearts. As you set the tone, hungering for a greater vision of God's glory in your own life, God can work through you to make your church hungry and thirsty for spiritual worship.

If you do not now have a daily private worship time, find five minutes today when you can be quiet before the Lord, read a short passage of the Bible and meditate on it, then praise the Lord for one thing. Increase this time daily by five minutes until you have reached your limit. You may want to also memorize a few choruses or a hymn and sing them to the Lord during your worship time, or while driving to work or while walking.

Devotional times with the family should be guided by the same principles. Periods of worship should be regular, but not so regulated as to disallow spontaneity or flexibility.

■ Discussion Questions ■

1. What are the different biblical meanings of the word "worship" and how should they relate to the way you worship?
2. What basics about worship did Jesus teach?
3. Why is corporate worship important?
4. What are some of the elements that should be included in the corporate worship service?
5. Why is individual worship important to your spiritual growth?
6. What is the concept of ACTS and how should it be applied to your private worship time?

■ Application Activities ■

1. Try to enter into every aspect of the worship service at your church. Apply the elements of the worship service to things coming up in the week ahead.
2. Think about your private devotion time. How much of that time is spent in worship? Practice the principles presented in this chapter during your devotion time.
3. Determine your spiritual gifts and how they can be used in worship that will minister to the body of Christ. Then, offer your gifts and talents to the worship service.
4. Have you ever been dissatisfied with the corporate worship at your church? List the things that you were dissatisfied with and constructive suggestions that would improve those things. Find a person with whom you can discuss these suggestions.

■ Bibliography ■

Allen, Ronald, and Borror, Gordon. *Worship, Rediscovering the Missing Jewel.* Portland, OR: Multnomah Press, 1982.

Ryrie, Charles C. *Basic Theology* Wheaton, IL: Victor Books, 1987.

Swindoll, Charles R. *Growing Deep in the Christian Life.* Portland, OR: Multnomah Press, 1986.

Tozer, A. W. *Whatever Happened to Worship?* Camp Hill, PA: Christian Publications, 1985.

Webber, Robert E. *Worship is a Verb.* Waco, TX: Word Books, 1985.

Wiersbe, Warren W. *Real Worship.* Nashville: Oliver-Nelson Books, 1986.

DETERMINING A
MEANINGFUL
CHURCH
RELATIONSHIP

7 Using the word "determining" in the title of this chapter draws attention to the basics or the origins of the church. Only from such a study can a model for personal church relationship be created. Similarly, the term "meaningful" suggests a relationship that produces important experiences and values and is much more than routine or habitual.

In the way it is used here, the term "relationship" suggests a dual obligation; both church and member are obligated to each other. Therefore, this chapter title has also defined the goal of its content. The outworking of this chapter in the believer's life is an important factor in growing toward spiritual maturity.

■ What is the church? ■

The true nature of the church has been subject to considerable confusion. Commonly, society sees church architecture and calls it the church of a particular city, region, or denomination. However, that structure is a building used by a church, not the church itself.

The organization and organism of God

Though men have designed many religious organizations, in his own time and in his own way, God fashioned his own design and called his particular organization—the church. Christ announced its coming to Peter in Matthew 16:18 when he said, "And I say also unto thee, That thou art Peter (Greek; *petros,* a stone), and upon this rock (Greek; *petra,* a large boulder) I will build my church; and the gates of hell shall not prevail against it." Thus, the church is initiated by God and is not only

54

an organization but an organism, for it comprises a living membership of believers, "Ye also, as living stones, are built up a spiritual house" (I Pet. 2:5).

Notice that the passage in Matthew clearly identifies that the basis of the church is the "rock" which is not Peter, for the Greek word for Peter means a stone or pebble, while the word translated "rock" means a large boulder. This large boulder is the church which comprises everyone (in this specific case, Peter and the disciples) who confess Christ as Lord.

A unique foundation

The church not only has the confession of Christ as Lord as a condition for membership, but its entire foundation is in Jesus Christ. Paul clearly states in many of his writings that the foundation of the church is Christ. In I Cor. 3:11 he says, "For other foundation can no man lay than that is laid, which is Jesus Christ," and Eph. 1:22,23, "And hath put all things under his feet, and gave him to be the head over all things to the church. Which is his body, the fulness of him that filleth all in all."

A model relationship

In Eph. 5:22,23 Paul compares the God-designed relationship between a husband and wife to Christ and his body—the church membership. Striking lessons of fidelity, love, faithfulness, and authority are shown to apply to both of these groups. As believers contemplate how husbands and wives should relate to each other, the real relationship that Christ seeks with each believer becomes clearer. Certainly, the reverse is also true, that is, the Head/church relationship becomes the model for ideal marriage.

A human institution

Though the church is a permanent, divine, never-destroyed creation of God, its membership is made up of fallible humans. Since religion has always fascinated people, they are often naturally attracted to becoming part of its membership though not truly confessing Christ as Lord and Savior. Therefore, the group of people meeting in a church building will include both imperfect saints and unbelievers with all their faults and weaknesses. Jesus provided insight to this condition in his parable of the tares (Matt. 13:36-43).

The ministry of the church

The Greek word which is translated "church" in the New Testament refers both to the local assembly of believers and a universal body of believers who have confessed Christ as Lord and Savior down through the centuries since the church began.

The term can be literally translated "called-out ones." This definition more clearly describes the true ministry of the church. Believers are "called out" from the world to live like their founder and head, Jesus

Christ. The church is God's people living the Christian life.

Even though believers receive a new nature at conversion, the old nature constantly seeks to reign supreme in their lives. The ministry of the church is to equip believers to overcome their old natures and to grow toward spiritual maturity.

Determining what the church is constitutes the first step in developing a meaningful relationship. Though the church has many pleasant and enjoyable functions, for a productive personal relationship the church must assure, as someone has quipped, that "the main thing is to keep the main thing the main thing." And, in this case, the "main thing" is equipping believers to live for Christ.

■ The believer's relationship to the church ■

Church history students have observed that the most vital periods in the history of the church were those when church members saw themselves as the "called-out ones" and aggressively propagated the gospel to a world in spiritual darkness. Conversely, the times when the church has been most ineffective have been when its members were satisfied to be spectators rather than participants in ministry.

Apostolic succession

The apostolic church is vividly seen in Acts 2 and provides today's believers with a clear pattern of God's intent for the church until Christ returns.

Since all believers today stand in apostolic succession to those who were at that first church meeting, that apostolic pattern and succession are still Christ's design for his church today.

Though Scripture allows for considerable creativity in its form, both historically and culturally, the function of the church is very clear and is the legacy of apostolic succession.

The lay person

According to apostolic practice, all ministry was carried out by laymen with the church leader providing the equipping for such lay service. One of the greatest reasons for the magnificent successes of the early church was the committed propagation and interactive ministry of its membership.

Though the term "laity" was not used in the first churches, it was used by Clement AD 95 and became the basis of the ministry of Francis of Assisi, Martin Luther, John Wycliffe, John Huss, and many others.

The New Testament makes no distinction between clergy and laity except in function. Clergy are not in a separate class, but are given special gifts and special roles. However, all believers are God's ministers and have unique spirit-given gifts to accomplish the ministry of the church. When church members awaken to this truth, identify their spiritual gifts, and undertake the ministry given them through apostolic succession, the church will once again turn this world "upside down" (Acts 17:6).

The priesthood of all believers

From the Reformation came Luther's great truth of the priesthood of all believers which awakened the sleeping church. This truth simply means that all believers are priests unto God. They have direct access and accountability to God.

Consequently, believers are God's priests to their world. Whatever God desires for society and each individual in that society, he has delegated to believers—his priests—to communicate his intent. Whatever God will do for society and each individual in that society, whether comfort, care, relief, or salvation, he intends his priests to be the means for accomplishing it. Christ touched upon this when he said, "Verily I say unto you, whatsoever ye shall bind on earth shall be bound in heaven: and whatsoever ye loose on earth shall be loosed in heaven" (Matt. 18:18).

When believers identify their appointment from God as apostolic succession, lay minister, and priest, they can no longer be satisfied to be mere spectators in the church, but are compelled to become active participants in ministry.

■ The believer's goals through the church ■

At the beginning of this chapter, it was stated that determining what the church is and what relationship believers have to that church were necessary before the word "meaningful" could be understood.

The New Testament's theme is that a satisfying and fulfilling relationship to the church will come only when believers are actively involved in biblical ministry.

Since ministry has frequently become so distorted in today's church, to insure accuracy, it is essential that ministry be defined by the Scripture. Though each of the following goals would profit from wider treatment, the purpose here is simply to list and explain each one. You are encouraged to study each of them and to begin applying and implementing them in your own personal ministry in a way that is consistent with your temperament, personality, and life-role.

World evangelization

The parting words of the Gospel according to Matthew record Christ's Great Commission (Matt. 28:18-20). Christ clearly intended this commission to be a personal goal for all believers. Claiming that it only applies to the clergy rather than the entire church is simply not scriptural. World evangelization is an essential part of God's formula for growing toward spiritual maturity. Seeking spiritual growth while ignoring evangelizing one's own sphere of influence is counter-productive.

Relational membership

The apostle Paul and others frequently used the term "one another" in their writings. By doing this, they stressed the highly relational design of the believer's ministry through and in the church.

Paul writes, "So we, being many, are one body in Christ, and every one members one of another" (Rom. 12:5). His analogy is that of the parts of the body and this theme reoccurs frequently (I Cor. 12, Rom. 12, and Eph. 4). When one part of the body suffers, the entire body suffers; when one part of the body rejoices, the entire body rejoices. In this church ministry injunction, the role of the growing believer is to be an active, functioning part of the body.

Devotional direction
The believer's devotion is to be directed toward other church family members as seen in Romans 12:10 (NASB), "Be devoted to one another in brotherly love." This is a very affectionate term and calls upon growing believers to fulfill their roles as affectionate family members one toward another.

Genuine honor
Making others look good is the theme of Romans 12:10, "In honour preferring one another." This is the role of the servant who in humility honors others whom he esteems to be of greater value than himself. How completely foreign this is to society's values. Yet, this is part of the formula for growing spiritually.

Unity
Scripture exhorts the believer to "be likeminded one toward another according to Christ Jesus" (Rom. 15:5). With this goal the growing Christian is to actively accept the role of unifier in interpersonal relationships.

Acceptance
The role of assimilator is the theme of "receive ye one another, as Christ also received us to the glory of God" (Rom. 15:7). In a world of bias and prejudice, satisfaction of this goal, even partially, places growing believers in an explosive ministry potential both inside and outside the church.

Admonishment
To balance the previous growth goal, Paul states, "And I myself also am persuaded of you, my brethren, that ye also are full of goodness, filled with all knowledge, able also to admonish one another" (Rom. 15:14). This is the role of confronting another who is involved in sin. Surely, this exhortation must be taken in light of the principles contained in I Cor. 13, the "love chapter." However, tolerating sin in the church is fatal to the spiritual growth of both the individual and the group.

Affectionate greetings
Though often misunderstood, Paul's instructions to "Greet one another with a holy kiss" (Rom. 16:16 NASB) actually is a spiritual growth ingredient that must not be ignored. The "holy kiss" was a cultural function of that day but the principle of expressing genuineness, care, and true concern to others in the church is yet true.

The casual, trivial, and superficial ways believers greet one another in churches today is anti-church as well as anti-personal spiritual growth.

Service
Throughout these goals the theme of service to others is paramount. Here, service also takes on added dimension when the Scripture states, "by love serve one another" (Gal. 5:13). The context of the passage argues for the freedom of the believer, while at the same time, calling for the serving of others in love. This is the role of the free slave, an interesting paradox in ministry.

Burden Bearing
The role of the restorer is seen in "Bear ye one another's burdens" (Gal. 6:2). Perhaps no other goal will require more prayer, tact, caution, and love than this. The restorer is truly fulfilling the priesthood role in this goal. And it is an unusual facet which produces spiritual growth.

Forgiving
Sounding similar to the previous goal, there is a difference when Paul states, "With all lowliness and meekness, with longsuffering, forbearing one another in love" (Eph. 4:2). Forgiveness of others links the growing believer with Christ in a fundamental manner and allows the grace of God to surface in the believer's life and ministry (Eph. 4:32).

Submitting
Becoming the yielder is the thrust of this ministry goal. Ephesians 5:21 declares "Submitting yourselves one to another in the fear of God." Yielders demonstrate their true status with Christ through this inter-relational ministry (Phil. 2:5-11).

Encouraging
Paul concludes this series of ministry goals by saying, "Therefore encourage one another and build each other up" (I Thess. 5:11 NIV). This may seem like a strange recipe for spiritual growth, yet it is the Scripture's premise that growth occurs interrelationally. Thus determining a meaningful church relationship is not simply the Christian's duty but is the very therapy that God uses to stimulate personal and corporate spiritual growth.

Interestingly as these goals are met, a dynamic and clear message is sent to the world. It sees a true church. It sees a divine relationship that it does not experience in the world and is strangely drawn to the believer's message of truth. True spiritual growth in the church as defined in these goals has always produced numerical church growth.

■ Summary ■
Determining what the true church is pointedly requires believers to define what their proper relationship should be. Since the church is

both the organization and organism of God, it provides a model relationship for man to God.

Recognizing that apostolic succession places special ministry obligations upon all believers, they look to the Scriptures for guidance in determining their ministry goals.

In the "one another" exhortations of the New Testament, a clear pattern is found. When these goals are being met, a fresh dynamic is unleashed in world evangelism and church love.

■ Discussion Questions ■

1. How does the believer's concept of the church differ from the unbeliever's?
2. What is the ministry of the church?
3. Why is the laity an important part of a church?
4. What obligations do you as a "priest of God" have?
5. Name the believer's goals through the church.

■ Application Activity ■

Following these steps will help you determine how well your church is fulfilling your personal ministry goals.

1. Identify church functions/activities that you attend and list them in a vertical column on a sheet of paper.
2. Evaluate each of these functions/activities to the goals cited in this chapter. List your observations in a vertical column on the right side of the page.
3. For those functions/activities which are questionable to your goals, begin to plan ways for eliminating them from your church experience.
4. Review other functions/activities of your church in which you are not now participating. Evaluate these in a similar way against your goals. Decide if any of these functions/activities could help you attain your goals and pledge to become a participant in those that will support your goals.
5. What functions/activities can you either bring into your church or influence their adoption which would better meet your goals?

■ Bibliography ■

Getz, Gene. *Building up One Another*. Wheaton, IL: Victor Books, 1976.

Sweeting, George. *The Basics of the Christian Life*. Chicago: Moody Press, 1983.

Treadwell, William, and McSwain, Larry. *Church Organization Alive*. Nashville: Broadman Press, 1987.

GROWING THROUGH MINISTRY

IDENTIFYING YOUR MINISTRY CAPABILITIES

8 One of the first lessons you must learn as a growing Christian is that you are saved to serve. You are not saved simply to satisfy yourself. You are saved by a sovereign Lord in order that he may use you in his plan for ministry in this universe. You have not been simply given a fire escape from hell. You have received the unique privilege of serving the most High God. And what a tremendous privilege that is!

To think that a sovereign God, who needs absolutely nothing in order to complete his plan for this world, carefully and divinely chooses each believer to be his means to accomplish that plan is simply supernatural. It is another demonstration of his grace toward his creatures. The same Lord who speaks and the worlds come into existence needs no mere human instrument to assist him in this magnificent task of sustaining the world. Yet, that is exactly what he has done. For Jesus said, "Ye have not chosen me, but I have chosen you, and ordained you, that ye should go and bring forth fruit" (John 15:16). Thus the Lord has chosen to delegate specific ministry tasks to all believers. And, to accomplish this ministry, he has given believers special gifts to make them effective.

■ What are the ministry gifts? ■

As soon as you begin considering ministry gifts, you must identify their source. Since, in this case, ministry gifts are being considered, it must be remembered that the gifts are given by the Spirit of God and not just some application of one's own endeavor or energy. Quite the contrary, that which is done in the energy of the flesh will certainly not accomplish the special goals that the Lord has in mind.

Paul says in Ephesians 4:11, 12, "And he gave some, apostles; and some, prophets; and some, evangelists; and some, pastors and teachers; for the perfecting of the saints, for the work of the ministry, for the edifying of the body of Christ." This passage makes it clear that God's purpose in giving gifts is to benefit the body of Christ. These gifts are not for building the ego or developing the power of the gift recipients. They are for ministry to the corporate body of believers. So whatever gifts believers have, the purpose of the gift is to benefit others and so glorify God.

Often Christians believe that they best glorify God by their ritual, be it church attendance, financial giving, or donating of their time in service. A careful reading of the Bible,however, demonstrates a plan quite different from such ritualism (Matt. 9:13; Isa. 1:11, etc.). This does not mean that church attendance, financial giving, and donating of time are not important. It does say that God is glorified best when believers are exercising their gifts in ministry to others.

Studying the outline below will help you better understand the doctrine of ministry gifts as the Bible presents it.

I. God intends that believers be wise concerning gifts (I Cor. 12:1)
   A. They are gifts (Rom. 1:11)
   B. They are special qualifications given by the Holy Spirit at the moment of conversion to enable the believer to serve best in the body of Christ
II. Every child of God has one or more gifts (I Cor. 12:7)
III. Personal gifts serve a very unique purpose (Eph. 4:11,12)
IV. Gifts make believers accountable to God (I Tim. 4:12,14)
V. Gifts are different from talents (I Pet. 4:11)
VI. Gifts are not to be confused with offices (apostle, prophet, etc.), ministries (a means to use that gift) or fruits (which have to do with the godliness of life)
VII. Spiritual gifts fall into three separate categories:
   A. The speaking gifts
      1. The apostolic gifts (Eph. 4:11), today's missionary gift.
      2. The gift of prophecy (Eph. 4:11), speaking forth for God through the means of testimony or declaration.
      3. The gift of evangelism (Eph 4:11), special abilities in communicating the gospel to unbelievers.
      4. The gift of teaching (Eph. 4:11), a unique ability to explain and apply the Word of God.
      5. The gift of exhortation (Rom. 12:8), a means of encouragement and comfort.
      6. The gift of knowledge and wisdom (I Cor. 12:8), the ability to have deep insight into the Word of God and its application to the problems of life.
   B. The serving gifts
      1. The gift of helps (I Cor. 12:28), the ability to serve the church in any supportive role.
      2. The gift of hospitality (I Pet. 4:9; Rom. 12:13), the special ability to provide an open house and warm welcome for those in need of food and lodging.
      3. The gift of giving (Rom. 12:8), more than tithing, this is the gift of delightful donation to the cause of Christ.

4. The gift of government (I Cor. 12:28), the special gift of leadership, whether lay or clerical.
5. The gift of showing mercy (Rom. 12:8), a gift of pity and action toward those who are needy.
6. The gift of faith (I Cor. 12:9), more than saving faith, this is the ability to see what God wants done and persevere through obstacles to completion.
7. The gift of discernment (I Cor. 12:10), an ability to distinguish between the Spirit of truth and the spirit of error.

C. The signifying gifts
1. The gift of miracles (I Cor. 12:10), the ability to cause supernatural and wonderful events to authenticate the divine commission.
2. The gift of healing (I Cor. 12:9), a supernatural ability to be instrumental in curing illness and restoring health.
3. The gift of tongues and interpretation (I Cor. 12:28), emitting ecstatic utterances and using or interpreting a foreign language unknown to either.

Many theologians disagree as to whether all of the above gifts are truly gifts and whether all of them are applicable to today. However, they are nonetheless the listing of the ministry gifts in the Bible that believers must reckon with when considering their own ministries.

Some of these gifts are much more common than others and, therefore; it is obvious that the Spirit of God intended that they be the most visible and active in the church. Unfortunately, it is possible for believers to become so enchanted by the more exotic gifts and spend undue time and energy seeking or discussing them that they miss God's most important priority for their personal ministries.

■ Which gifts do you have? ■

This is the big question for many believers. Unfortunately when you were saved, God did not emblazon upon your forehead the citation of your gifts. He did this for a good reason. For in the process of exploring your gifts as a new believer, your spiritual life prospers and grows.

Use these guidelines as you begin determining your spiritual gifts: discover your strengths, determine your weaknesses, consult Christian friends, and use the process of trial and error to identify where they feel you are successful.

Discover your strengths

The first step in determining your spiritual gifts is to try to discover your strengths. In doing this, you must be careful to screen out those strengths or successes that are most likely due to your own native talent or learned skills. What you need to discover here are those victories, successes, and strengths in your attempts at ministry that seem to go beyond any natural explanation. Think about those events and circumstances that produced success, victory, or strength that can only be attributed to some supernatural source. Discovering these events will be the key to your spiritual gift(s).

Determine your weaknesses

The second step is to determine your weaknesses. Following the above theme, evaluate why other events seemed not to work out well as you attempted to minister. As you uncover these failures, evidences of ineffectiveness, or weaknesses in your ministry attempts, a pattern will emerge which will reveal those gifts that God has not given you.

Consult Christian friends

To give further insight on your spiritual gifts, it is helpful to consult with Christian friends who know you well and have observed you during times when you have been ministering. For this to be effective, you must find friends who are themselves maturing Christians. Only these individuals have the ministry of the Holy Spirit within them and can assist you in your search. These believers must also be close friends that will be comfortable sharing with you objectively.

Use the process of trial and error

In pursuit of identifying your ministry gifts, some trial and error will be necessary. As an old wise saying states, "the carpenter who does not make chips does not make anything else, either." Thus, you will need to make many attempts at ministry to find a revealing pattern which will enable you to focus on the gifts that will best benefit you in serving the kingdom of God.

■ When do you employ your gifts? ■

A serious problem in today's churches is that program staff are recruited and placed into service before either the leadership or the program staff have identified their ministry gifts. Such efforts, regardless of how well-intentioned, produce mediocrity, for it is at cross-purposes to the Spirit of God. The Lord has promised believers that he will give sufficient gifts to his children in order that the church can effectively accomplish his mission. In his wisdom, the Lord has given gifts to believers according to his own divine insight which is designed to make the church successful in its ministries.

Once your ministry gifts have been determined, the next step is personal commitment. These are *your* gifts and, therefore, God will hold *you* accountable to carry them out. Hence, these gifts need to be a high priority for devoting your energy. These gifts are not optional. They are part of God's divine plan for your ministry in the church.

Developing your gifts is also part of your commitment. When you receive your gifts from the Lord, they are usually somewhat primitive and in need of considerable development and usage in order to make them as effective as he wants them to be. Therefore those gifts that your heavenly Father gave you are his investment in you which he expects will pay rich dividends when fully developed.

Developing your gifts is an on-going, lifetime commitment. To stay abreast of new technology and information that becomes available, you should be taking courses, reading new books, and attending seminars and conferences. This is called lifelong education.

Another serious problem facing the church is that program staff are using obsolete and ineffective skills in the light of today's knowledge and technology. It is not that most believers refuse to develop their gifts further, but they often do not realize that it is necessary to do so. Developing your gifts is essential as you continue to grow toward spiritual maturity.

Returning to the question, "When do you employ your gifts?" Remembering three words will help—anticipate, adapt, and act. This threefold process should guide you as you contemplate the support ministry that God wants you to employ.

Anticipate

Begin by anticipating such circumstances in your family, on the job, in your social life, in addition to your spiritual life, that will have an effect on employing your spiritual gifts.

Adapt

Adapting requires that you fit your gift into your unique experiences and opportunities for service. Again, this is where many believers miss good opportunities of ministry. Even though circumstances differ slightly from previous experiences in using your gift(s), don't fail to recognize other potential opportunities for employing your ministry gift(s).

Adapting means that you are flexible enough to fit into situations that vary widely in scope and still serve Christ effectively. Adapting requires you to depend upon the Spirit of God for guidance and leadership in such uncharted areas. But it can also be one of your greatest challenges as a believer.

Act

Though you anticipate opportunities for employing your spiritual gifts and adapt to the changing settings for service, before anything happens you need to act. It is too easy to speculate and philosophize about service and yet never become active.

The human mind and spirit often allows people to become self-satisfied simply by considering and taking a stand on the issue without ever becoming involved. Without taking action, the previous efforts are just cerebral gymnastics. Your enemy, Satan, is delighted with such tactics. To be sure, action without purposes or goals can be misplaced action. The point here is that after you have considered all the details of serving the Lord through your ministry gifts, you need to take action.

But where does this action take place? The Bible says that believers are both members of this world and citizens of heaven. Thus, the world is your present stage for ministry. You are not limited to the local church, however, though it should be the focus of your ministry. Believers need to constantly remind themselves that they are *global* as well as *local* Christians. Such awareness adds thrilling scope to your life. To think that Jesus has specially gifted you and seeks to use you in unique ways in this world is indeed thrilling!

■ Summary ■

Identifying your ministry gifts is a very important part of your continued maturing in Christ. By using your Spirit-given gifts in ministry to others, you are contributing to the body of Christ and glorifying God. The wide variety of gifts identified in the Bible are an indication of the diversity of people's needs. A thoughtful examination of your life and consultation with other believers will help you to discover your ministry gifts. After identifying these gifts, you must be concerned with developing them and employing them in service for your Lord.

■ Discussion Questions ■

1. What is the difference between ministry gifts and talents?
2. What guidelines should you follow in determining your gifts?
3. What are some ways in which you can develop your gifts?
4. How are anticipation, adaptation, and action used in employing your spiritual gifts?

■ Application Activities ■

1. Using your Bible, research the ministry gifts outlined in this chapter and then identify through your concordance the applications of those gifts. Use this research as a basis for identifying your spiritual gift(s).
2. Develop a support group that is feasible and workable to your time and location demands. This group should be 3-4 persons who will explore ministry gifts together, identifying as well as assisting each other in developing those gifts in ministry settings. This group should plan and commit to weekly meetings for at least 6 months.

■ Bibliography ■

Baxter, Ronald E. *Gifts of the Spirit.* Grand Rapids, MI: Kregel Publications, 1983.

Gangel, Kenneth O. *Unwrap Your Spiritual Gifts.* Wheaton, IL: Victor Books, 1983.

Jones, R. Wayne. *Using Spiritual Gifts.* Nashville: Broadman Press, 1985.

Kinghorn, Kenneth C. *Gifts of the Spirit.* Nashville: Abingdon Press, 1976.

Lutzer, Erwin W. *You're Richer Than You Think!* Wheaton, IL: Victor Books, 1978.

McRae, William. *The Dynamics of Spiritual Gifts.* Grand Rapids, MI: Zondervan Publishing House, 1983.

MINISTERING
THROUGH
EVANGELISM
AND CARE

9 Once you have determined what your ministry gifts are, you need to make them priorities in serving the Lord. Your spiritual gifts will be the major emphasis of your life ministry as a global Christian. For example, some believers will make teaching the major emphasis in ministry, for others it will be administration or preaching, etc. There are some areas, however, in which the Lord expects all believers to minister in addition to their gifted areas.

Among these areas are evangelism and care-giving. Believers should not assume that because some have been given specific gifts in evangelism or care-giving that God intends for only those persons to minister in these ways. On the contrary, even though some have been given special gifts in these areas and that they make them their major ministry for the Lord, all believers have responsibility for evangelizing and care-giving.

It is true that some believers have been given the gift of evangelism (Eph. 4:11), but Christ also commanded every believer to witness, proclaim the gospel, and make disciples as seen in Matthew 28:19,20, "Go ye therefore, and teach all nations, baptizing them in the name of the Father, and the Son, and the Holy Ghost: teaching them to observe all things whatsoever I have commanded you: and lo, I am with you always, even unto the end of the world."

The same exhortation is given in Mark 16:15, Matthew 13:52, and Acts 1:8. Proverbs 11:30 also corroborates it, "he that winneth souls is wise." Thus, evangelism is not an option; the Lord makes it clear that he expects all believers to evangelize.

The essence of evangelism is proclaiming the good news that Christ paid the penalty for sin and that if sinners will by faith repent and believe, Christ will change their lives to conform to his example. All believers can witness to this truth or the Lord would not have commanded them to do it.

God has empowered some persons to be evangelists and has blessed their efforts by giving them success. Even though other believers are not gifted in this manner, Christ still expects them to witness to his saving power.

■ Why are these ministeries considered together? ■

While it would seem that evangelism and care-giving are separate areas of ministry, there are good reasons to link them together.

The Bible links them

The ministry of evangelism and care-giving are considered together in this chapter because the Bible links them. God expects Christians to care for others in both of these ways. You should not think of evangelism as simply proclaiming the truth regardless of societal response. Nothing is clearer in the Bible than that God expects all believers to be caregivers of their fellow citizens of this world. Jesus demonstrated this to his disciples over and over again during his three-year ministry.

Evangelism results from caring

Without genuine care motivating the believer, true evangelism cannot be properly carried out. Caring is the main force which drives believers to share with others what Christ has done in their lives.

Another motivation is that true believers care about other persons' needs. Though believers are to be jealous for the truth, the motive that will make the greatest impact upon unbelievers is sharing the gospel witness in response to meeting their demonstrated needs.

Evangelism and care always interface

To begin considering the ministry of care, you need to highlight the gifts listed in the previous chapter under "serving gifts." Obviously there are functions of the other gifts that also reflect caring (for example, healing or miracles), but it is clearer to use the category of "serving gifts" as a basic understanding of what is meant by care.

Particularly the areas of "helps, hospitality, giving and showing mercy" emphasize this ministry of care-giving. Certainly these ministry areas can and will at times be administered without evangelizing the care-recipient. But the concern here, however, is to show that when evangelism in done in a biblical fashion it always interfaces with care-giving.

■ What impact can I have? ■

The inscription on Confucius' tomb reads "He teaches for 10,000 years." Considering the average lifespan today that seems rather impressive. For believers who are involved in ministries of evangelism and care, however, their impact is for eternity not just for 10,000 years.

With world population growing at a rapid pace (some statisticians suggest that the present population will more than triple in the next 25 years), the need for evangelism has never been greater. Only as believers realize their responsibility in the ministry of evangelism and care will Christ's mission be adequately perpetuated in this population explosion.

Jude demonstrated the unique relationship between evangelism and care when he said "And of some having compassion, making a difference" (verse 22). In order for the church of Jesus Christ to effectively evangelize such an expanding population, evangelism attempts will need to be conducted in compassion (care), which according to the Scriptures will make a difference.

■ What techniques should I use? ■

There are a multitude of systems, formulas, or laws available to believers. A very simple, yet tremendously powerful tool often called the "Roman Road" is found in the book of Romans. Each of the verses are sequential and beautifully designed to help believers present Christ's plan of salvation to unbelievers. Keep in mind, however, that whatever approach is used, it should be done in a ministry of care.

The "Roman Road" begins with Romans 3:10 with its declaration that "there is none righteous, no, not one." Supporting this first step is 3:23, "for all have sinned and come short of the glory of God." This first step strips unbelievers of any self-righteousness before God. A second step is the need to identify unbelievers with Adam's sin found in 5:17. This confirms that everyone has inherited Adam's sinful nature.

In 6:23 unbelievers are confronted with the gift that is theirs if they will accept it by faith, "for the wages of sin is death but the gift of God is eternal life through Jesus Christ our Lord." This is the third step. From that passage the evangelist can take unbelievers to 10:9,10, the fourth step, which reads, "that if thou confess with thy mouth the Lord Jesus, and shalt believe in thine heart that God hath raised him from the dead, thou shalt be saved. For with the heart man believeth unto righteousness; and with the mouth confession is made unto salvation."

Thus, in a series of short, clear passages in one book of the Bible, you can lead other persons to a saving knowledge of Jesus Christ. Throughout all evangelism efforts there should be a quality of friendship as well as boldness, a truthfulness as well as a recognition of the personal needs of the other person. As always, the most effective ministry will be found when you have wholly yielded yourself to the Holy Spirit's power to influence that other person.

■ Where should I begin? ■

The apostolic pattern of the New Testament is seen in Acts 1:8 when the Lord said, "ye shall be witnesses unto me both in Jerusalem, and in all Judea, and Samaria, and unto the uttermost part of the earth." This pattern is likened to ever-increasing circles when you drop a pebble in a pool. The beginning point is always the area that is closest to the point of impact. For many that may be your family and it can be where you witness most effectively. Yet, the Lord cautioned that your family can also be the location of your greatest defeats in evangelism (Matthew 13:57).

From your "Jerusalem" you need to move out to your "Samaria" and the remotest parts of the world. When you accept the Acts 1:8 injunction as your biblical pattern for evangelism and caring, many priorities immediately become quite clear. For example, you then realize that home missions must be the beginning point of your ministry of evangelism and care-giving and then it branches out to foreign missions. Today this pattern often becomes distorted and the thrust of evangelism efforts get reversed.

Statisticians now tell us that in the next 25 years, there will be a phenomenal growth of what they term "mega-cities." These cities will house millions of inhabitants and be the logical focus of some of Christianity's most effective evangelism. Many of these cities will be either in Central or South America.

■ How should I evaluate my ministry? ■

Perhaps the most essential element of your evangelism and caring ministry is evaluating whether it has been both efficient and effective.

Efficiency and effectiveness

The concepts of efficiency and effectiveness are different. Being *efficient* means doing "things right," while being *effective* means doing "right things."

To help make this clearer, consider these examples: You are being *efficient* when you focus on your attempts at evangelizing and caring and continue to modify them so that these tasks are being accomplished as well as they possibly can. But you are being *effective* when you look at the ways you have attempted to evangelize and give care and challenge whether they are the best use of your resources.

Effectiveness, then, is concerned with whether you are properly using your resources to achieve your goals. Being effective will allow you to redirect your energy and resources to accomplish only those tasks which help you achieve your goals of evangelizing and care-giving. That may require that you discontinue some tasks that you have been doing.

It is possible to fail in your ministry by only being efficient or effective. You need to be careful to use your ministry gifts in such a manner that they produce both efficiency and effectiveness. That will take diligence on your part; but the Lord expects growing Christians to be diligent.

Outcomes of ministry

You also need to assess your evangelism and caring ministry in the light of its outcomes as well as its inputs. You can easily concentrate on what you are doing (input) and minimize what others are doing as a consequence (output). Both are important, however. Since your role in evangelism and caring is being stressed here, you could easily slide into an unbalanced emphasis upon the input side of ministry. What is just as important is for you to assess whether the effects (outcomes) of your ministry of evangelism and care-giving are, in fact, resulting in people coming to know Christ.

Surely, when these outcomes are not happening, you need to correct your inputs to insure they will better contribute to reaching your goals.

Internal versus external efforts

There is a third area of contrast that you need to consider in evaluating your ministry of evangelism and care. You need to place that ministry against the backdrop of internal versus external efforts. This means that your ministry assessment has to consider both what you are doing in the church and what you are doing in society. This is the global concept of the Christian that was discussed earlier.

■ Summary ■

This chapter has stressed that you, as a growing and maturing Christian, need to be a good steward of the ministry gifts that God has given you and also should obey Christ's commands to all believers in the area of evangelism and care-giving. To accomplish this you need to evaluate your ministry against efficiency as well as effectiveness, against outcome as well as input, and against internal as well as external efforts.

This is part of your role in the priesthood of the believer. And it is highly motivating to realize that God has sovereignly given these gifts and injunctions to use in his world and that one day he will call for an accounting of such ministry. I Corinthians 3:12-18 teaches that all believers will be accountable for all of what they do in their lives, not just specific acts of piety in the church. In these verses Paul never used the term "works" (plural), but always the singular form "work" denoting a believer's entire life ministry.

Thus, an essential factor in your pilgrimage of growing toward spiritual maturity will be recognizing and balancing your ministry gifts with the common injunctions of ministering in the areas of evangelism and care as well as the employing of them throughout life. This indeed is stewardship.

■ Discussion Questions ■

1. Why are evangelism and care-giving two areas of ministry in which all Christians must be involved?
2. What is the link between evangelism and care-giving?
3. What is the "Roman Road?" Make an outline of this technique.
4. How can the apostolic pattern set forth in Acts 1:8 be adapted to your own situation?
5. What is the difference between being "efficient" and being "effective?" How should they be used in evaluating your evangelism and care-giving ministry?
6. Why must you be sensitive to the outcomes of your ministry?

■ Application Activities ■

1. Develop a support group of three or four believers for the purpose of mutual encouragement in the ministry of evangelism and care. This

group should meet weekly or biweekly to share testimonies regarding evangelism and caring and to motivate each other to continue and expand this ministry.

2. In your personal devotional life, be alert for the examples of how Christ linked evangelism and caring. Pledge to make some of these examples models that you will seek to emulate.

■ Bibliography ■

Innes, Dick. *I Hate Witnessing.* Ventura, CA: Regal Books, 1985.

Little, Paul E. *How to Give Away Your Faith.* Downers Grove, IL: InterVarsity Press, 1966.

Miles, Delos. *Overcoming Barriers to Witnessing.* Nashville: Broadman Press, 1984.

Petersen, Jim. *Evangelism as a Lifestyle.* Colorado Springs: NavPress, 1980.

Rinker, Rosalind. *You Can Witness with Confidence.* Grand Rapids, MI: Zondervan Publishing House, 1984.

Sweeting, George. *How to Witness Successfully.* Chicago: Moody Press, 1978.

MINISTERING

THROUGH

TEACHING

10 Growing spiritually involves serving God through ministry to people. Christians are to search for opportunities to serve. As the Scriptures say, "let us have grace, whereby we may serve God acceptably" (Heb. 12:28). This service, however, cannot earn salvation, rather, such ministry to people is a grateful expression to God through Jesus Christ.

Spiritual life and growth must be viewed as a result of God's grace. The Scripture states this clearly, "For by grace are ye saved" (Eph. 2:8). Expressions of spiritual growth, such as teaching or other acts of spiritual service, provide a way for believers to "shew forth the praises of him who hath called you out of darkness into his marvellous light" (I Peter 2:9).

As believers grow in grace there is a corresponding growth in gratitude. Spiritual service, such as being active in the ministry of a local church, provides a way to give grateful thanksgiving to Jesus Christ.

Teaching and learning in the church are simply ways of showing gratefulness to God and growing in relationship to God and man. Teaching, for example, does not always need to be thought of in the professional sense of the word (as with school teachers) or from the point of view that only those who are uniquely, spiritually-gifted may teach (as in Romans 12:7; I Cor. 12:28; and Eph. 4:11). Rather, in many different ways, all Christians who are growing spiritually will be involved in teaching God's Word. Christ's commission found in Matt. 28:18-20 was not given exclusively to those who are instructors in formal classroom situations. Jesus commissioned all believers to "Go . . . and teach all nations."

What the Bible refers to as teaching in passages like Deut. 6:7 and Heb. 5:12 should happen in normal, everyday communication. As parents tell their children about spiritual things and as believers discuss the Word of God together, biblical teaching takes place. Such teaching occurs through the natural, spontaneous, and constant talking about the Lord. Of course, this kind of teaching is also carried out in a more formal manner through the Sunday school or other church educational ministries. But these educational ministries need not be thought of as the only places spiritual teaching takes place.

■ What teaching is ■

As mentioned earlier, teaching is what Christians should do naturally as they live and witness in the world. Teaching goes on continually. It happens when families open the Word together around the dinner table or perhaps before bedtime. Teaching happens when one person gives or receives spiritual advice from another. Teaching occurs when an unbeliever hears the gospel while being witnessed to and, in faith and repentance, accepts Christ as Savior and Lord. But teaching also happens in more formal ways in the classrooms of churches and Christian schools as trained teachers use lesson-planning skills and effective teaching techniques. In every situation where teaching results in spiritual growth, the transforming power of the gospel is being experienced.

Whether the Word of God is taught informally through everyday living or in more organized ways through classroom instruction, it is through teaching the Word that God transforms the lives of people in the world. Lois LeBar, in her book *Focus on People in Church Education,* points out the impact of teaching the Word. "It is a bridge from the Word to the world. It is combining the *what* and *how* of the Lord's work. Christian education is discovering how the Spirit of God, the divine Teacher, works and working with Him. It is allowing the Word of God to transform every area of life. It is making disciples of all nations."

Teaching is sharing

It is an experience shared between a teacher and learners with the teacher guiding and directing the process. Because the church is described in Scripture as a place of unity, fellowship, and communion; teaching must be interactive and participative.

Whether informally as parents and children discuss how the Lord has blessed and cared for them in good and bad times or, more formally, as believers share around a particular verse of Scripture, interaction helps clarify God's truth and apply it to life situations.

Teaching is an active process

People learn by what they do and by the kind of experiences they have with others. As students are involved with each other and with the teacher, their relationship to Jesus Christ is developed. As fellow believers learn to share their inner feelings and learn to empathize and sympathize with each other, they are better able to understand their true relationship to Jesus Christ. It is for this reason that the first and foremost characteristic of Christian teachers must be their relationship to Jesus Christ.

Teaching is for life change

Teaching and learning involve more than knowing the facts found in Scripture. The result of the process is to have an effect on the whole person: intellect, attitudes, and behavior. The ideal result of teaching is seen in the way Christ grew during childhood. "Jesus increased in wisdom (mental development) and stature (physical development), and in favor with God (spiritual development) and man (social development)" (Luke 2:52). Teaching must be directed toward helping people experience the Word for themselves in all areas of their development. The Bible should be taught so that it relates to all of life.

■ Jesus the teacher ■

In many places and situations Jesus is addressed as "teacher." In fact, in the gospels, Jesus is referred to as a teacher more than by any other title.

He was called teacher

The Greek word most often given to Christ as an educational title is usually translated "teacher" or "master" and is found more than forty times in the gospels. Most frequently in the King James Version of the Bible this word is translated "master," rather than "teacher" because, at the time of translation, the word "master" was understood to mean "schoolmaster."

Not only did Jesus' disciples refer to him as teacher or master (Mark 4:38), but the scribes and Pharisees referred to him in this way as well. For example, Nicodemus said, "We know that thou art a teacher come from God" (John 3:2). Also, Jesus identified himself by the term "teacher." When he sent two of his followers to find the room for the Last Supper, he instructed the disciples to say, "The Master (teacher) saith, 'where is the guestchamber where I shall eat the passover with my disciples?'" (Mark 14:14).

Other Bible passages also point out the priority of teaching in the ministry of Christ. Examples of these are "Jesus went about all Galilee, *teaching* in the synagogues" (Matt. 4:23), "He opened his mouth, and *taught* them" (Matt. 5:2), and "he *taught* them as one having authority" (Matt. 7:29).

"Rabbi" is another title associated with the word teacher and used to refer to Christ. This word is also sometimes translated "master." The word "Rabbi" is a Jewish title that designated one as able to teach with the authority of Moses and having authority to interpret the law. Nicodemus and the disciples of John the Baptist called Jesus "Rabbi" (John 1:38; 3:2). "Rabboni," a similar but even more intensively educational and relational title, was used to refer to Christ by Mary Magdalene in addressing him when he appeared to her after the resurrection (John 20:16).

He taught through many different situations

When selected Scripture passages are examined, it becomes obvious that Christ taught in a variety of group situations. Three scriptural examples of his teaching illustrate this: one-on-one, small groups, and large crowds. The conversation between Christ and the Samaritan woman (John 4:1-42) is an instance of *one-on-one* teaching. In this passage Jesus meets a woman while standing at the well in Samaria. The result of Jesus interacting with the woman is seen in her learning about the "life-giving water." The conversation included an application with Christ saying, "whosoever drinketh of the water that I shall give him shall never thirst" (v. 14). The woman responded, "Sir, give me this water" (v. 15).

Jesus celebrating the Lord's Supper with his disciples in the upper room illustrates *small group* learning (Luke 22:14-38). In fact, many of the small group learning situations took place between Jesus and his disciples. In this case, as the disciples were alone with Christ discussing the coming days and eating a meal; they learned about his sacrifice and betrayal, their place in the kingdom, and Peter's denial of Christ. The time they spent together resulted in a new awareness on their part about Christ's work and how they were to serve him.

Christ continually taught *large groups* of people who constantly followed him. One of the many large group learning situations in Scripture occurred when the multitudes heard him denounce the scribes and Pharisees (Matt. 23:1-39). Here, clearly organized and powerfully presented information was given to teach the multitudes to do what the scribes and Pharisees said but not what they did. After condemning their hypocritical leadership, Christ concluded with the life application of "Blessed is he that cometh in the name of the Lord" (v. 39).

Believers today are responsible to continue the Lord's teaching ministry, whether in large groups, small groups, or through one-on-one interaction. Christians are to be involved in the ministry that Jesus "began both to do and teach" (Acts 1:1). His followers are to realize that the gospel is spread through obedience to the Great Commission's "teaching them to observe all things whatsoever I have commanded you" (Matt. 28:20). Christ-like living and a desire to continue to grow and mature in him will lead you to be a teacher of the gospel message whether in formal settings in classrooms or informally with family, friends, neighbors, or associates.

■ How to be an effective teacher ■

Christ has been described as teacher. His example in teaching and the commission that he gave to teach have been identified. Based upon this foundation, consider the following principles and personal qualities that will help you teach effectively.

Frank E. Gaebelein, a noted Christian educator, gave one of the best descriptions of what it means to be effective at teaching in whatever situation. His principles are as follows.

Principles for effective teaching

First, people who are *open and bold in witnessing* to their Christian faith will be effective in teaching. These are believers who are able to say with the apostle Paul, "I am not ashamed of the gospel of Christ" (Romans 1:16). This means that those who are effective at teaching look for opportunities to share their faith. Whether at work, home, or church, they do not hold back their enthusiasm and excitement for Jesus Christ.

Second, those who are effective at teaching *know the Bible.* This means that the Bible must be read and studied daily, not just at church or when it is convenient. Training classes often help believers better understand the Word and know how to teach it effectively. God's Word is relevant for all of life and learning. Those who are effective at teaching affirm that "All Scripture is given by inspiration of God and is profitable for doctrine, for reproof, for correction, for instruction in righteousness" (II Tim. 3:16).

Third, those who are effective teachers have to be *thoroughly committed to the truth.* Teachers' lives should reflect honesty and uprightness. Because those doing the teaching are examples to their learners, they must stand for truth, without compromise, in every area of daily living.

Fourth, those who are effective in teaching *strive for excellence.* God is not satisfied with mediocrity. He is full of glory and perfect in all his ways. As image-bearers of God, teachers and learners should seek to glorify him with their thoughts, attitudes, and actions. Thorough preparation, quality teaching, and caring relationships result from a desire to achieve excellence.

Fifth, believers who are effective at teaching *love others.* Children, youth, and adults are precious to Jesus Christ. They should be appreciated and cared about by anyone who teaches in a Christ-like way. Loving others means understanding the impact of sin and temptation on their lives, realizing everyone's need to have a saving relationship with Jesus Christ, and being willing to spend time with these people to build spiritually-supportive relationships. Sometimes people enjoy telling others the facts of Scripture so much that they neglect how these facts relate and apply to the lives of those they are teaching. Both the information and the application of God's Word must be given equal importance. The Scripture directs Christians to be "speaking the truth in love" (Eph. 4:15).

Finally, those who are effective at teaching are *wholly submitted to Jesus Christ—the greatest teacher.* God said this very clearly, "This is my beloved Son, in whom I am well pleased; hear ye him" (Matt 17:5). This concept requires a life of commitment and discipleship. Either Christ is Lord of all or he is not Lord at all. Effective Christian teachers are to be willing to be led by their Lord, whatever the cost. Many who are teachers will tell you that, of themselves, they would never have become involved in teaching. But, they responded to the opportunity to minister and the call of their teacher, Jesus Christ.

Personal qualities for effective teaching

In addition to the above six points, many Scripture passages name more qualities that should be found in all who teach. These include having a personality that is accepting, encouraging, patient, reasonable, not a gossip, faithful, sets a worthy example, is resourceful, loving, wise, and gentle.

Cautions are given in James 3 and 4 about taking the responsibilities of teaching seriously. In these chapters James makes it clear that Christians, especially teachers, are to be careful about how they communicate. They should speak so as not to offend others, and live in purity with no bitterness, envy, strife, lying, partiality, or hypocrisy; being pure, peaceable, gentle, open, merciful, and fruitful.

■ Summary ■

Spiritual growth is related to teaching and sharing with others in this chapter. Life in Christ also involves learning from him and serving him. Growth, in addition, requires that you obediently share God's Word, following Christ's example as teacher. He imparted the truth. One way for you to continue to grow and mature as a Christian is to follow the example of Jesus Christ by serving him through the ministry of teaching.

■ Discussion Questions ■

1. What is the relationship between spiritual growth and teaching?

2. Why should you, as a growing and maturing Christian, be interested in spiritual growth including teaching?

3. Name some ways that all believers are teachers as they live and witness in the world.

4. In what ways does teaching enable the Word of God to transform lives?

5. Of the three aspects of teaching described in the chapter, which do you think is of greatest importance? Why?

■ Application Activities ■

1. Look up the Bible references given in this chapter that refer to Christ as teacher. Read the references in their context and list what each passage says about Christ, the characteristics of teaching each describes, and what the Lord requires as a result of what is taught in the passage.

2. Identify a Christian teacher who you respect and ask the person if you may observe the class he/she teaches. During the observation take note of the principles and personal qualities that you observe in this person.

■ Bibliography ■

Coleman, Lucien E. *Why the Church Must Teach*. Nashville: Broadman Press, 1984.

Gangel, Kenneth O. *Understanding Teaching*. Wheaton, IL: Evangelical Teacher Training Association, 1968.

Held, Ronald G. *Learning Together.* Springfield, MO: Gospel Publishing, 1976.

Joy, Donald M. *Meaningful Learning in the Church.* Winona Lake, IN: Light and Life Press, 1969.

LeBar, Lois E. *Education That is Christian.* Old Tappan, NJ: Revell, 1981.

_____. *Focus on People in Church Education.* Old Tappan, NJ: Revell, 1968.

MINISTERING

THROUGH

LEADERSHIP

All Christians who are truly growing spiritually will be involved in leadership. While there are varying degrees of leadership, being one of God's people always requires some responsibility for the leading of others. Since there are so many different ways in which leadership can be exercised, all Christians should be able to find satisfying leadership roles in the home, church, and society.

| 11 |

The Scriptures require leadership responsibility in all areas of life. For example, leadership must take place in the home. Parents are to teach God's commands faithfully to their children. Parental leadership is required in the Old and New Testaments. Through Moses, God said to the Israelites, "thou shalt teach them diligently unto thy children and shalt talk of them (God's commands) when thou sittest in thine house, and when thou walkest by the way, and when thou liest down, and when thou risest up" (Deut. 6:7). In the New Testament, parents are told to lead their children in the "nurture and admonition of the Lord" (Ephesians 6:4).

The Scriptures describe the church as a body with each member of the body responsible for functioning "as God hath dealt to every man the measure of faith" (Rom. 12:3). There are enough leadership opportunities in the church for every believer. Opportunities range from giving hospitality to the exhortation associated with preaching.

Society, if it is to be positively influenced for Christ, needs to see the moral and ethical value of spiritual leadership in all areas of life. And Christian leadership in society must be through the believer's life and witness. Even in early society in Genesis, Adam and Eve were charged with having dominion (or authority) over the creation. God said, "let them have dominion over the fish of the sea, and over the fowl of the air, and over the cattle, and over all the earth" (Genesis 1:26). Psalm 8 also refers to people as having "dominion over the works of thy (God's) hands" (v. 6). In addition, Jesus described the leadership role of believers as being "the salt of the earth" and "the light of the world" so that others might see their good works and glorify God (Matt. 5:13-16).

Leadership responsibility is required of every believer, not just selected individuals. Through leadership in the home, church, and society, you, as a growing and maturing Christian, should function as a savoring salt and a shining light.

■ Leadership defined ■

Leading, from a Christian perspective, is an activity that involves influencing and directing the lives of others in a Christ-like way and applying the principles given in the Scriptures. Leadership is the using of one's God-given gifts and abilities in loving service to a person or group for the sake of Christ. The result of biblical leadership is the growth of individuals and groups in Christ-likeness toward the upbuilding and outreaching of the church and kingdom of Christ.

■ Jesus' principles of leadership ■

A study of the life of Christ reveals the characteristic of his emphasis on leadership. These principles provide a model for the believer seeking to grow in a spiritual sense.

The authority of Scripture

The rabbis of Old Testament times had distorted God's Word. Christ pointed out the errors of their teaching and the correct interpretation by saying, "Ye have heard that it was said . . . But I say unto you" (Matt. 5:21-23).

The importance of his person and work

Christian leadership cannot be separated from the work that Jesus came to do as Saviour and Lord. He said, "the Son of man is come to seek and to save that which was lost" (Luke 19:10).

The early church affirmed Jesus' absolute authority, "God hath made that same Jesus, whom ye have crucified, both Lord and Christ" (Acts 2:36).

The importance of individuals

Jesus focused upon individuals growing spiritually and taking responsibility for ministry.

When the disciples were called, they were men who had little or no training. Their only ability seemed to be their availability to be used by Christ. Jesus, therefore, concentrated his ministry on developing these disciples. By the time of his departure, he was able to charge them with carrying on his work saying, "Ye shall be witnesses unto me both in Jerusalem, and in all Judea, and in Samaria, and unto the uttermost part of the earth" (Acts 1:8).

It is exciting to consider the incredible growth that the disciples must have experienced during the approximately three-and-one-half years of

Christ's earthly ministry. To be transformed from a fisherman on the Sea of Galilee to a witness to all nations is thrilling. Such was the importance of individuals to Jesus.

The purposefulness of his life and ministry

Jesus testified that he came to accomplish a particular purpose. "I must work the works of him that sent me" (John 9:4). From the beginning to the end of the New Testament, the saving purpose of the ministry of Christ is clear. Matthew begins with "he shall save his people from their sins" (Matt. 1:21). Revelation ends with "I Jesus have sent mine angel to testify unto you these things in the churches . . . whosoever will, let him take of the water of life freely" (Rev. 22:16,17).

Christ-like leadership, of course, must be patterned after the life of our Lord. Therefore, the authority of Scripture will be respected. The person and work of Christ will be central. And ministry will focus on the equipping of individuals for spiritual service that is directed toward bringing the message of repentance and faith in Christ. Recognizing the leadership qualities of Christ provides a foundation for the principles of New Testament leadership for Christian leaders today.

■ Characteristics of Christian leaders ■

Christian leaders are known through the many ways that they function and relate to others. Five key characteristics of biblical leadership are essential to personal growth: servanthood, service, caring, delegation, and encouragement.

Servanthood

Christ is often seen in Scripture as a servant. One of the best known passages on servant leadership occurs when the mother of James and John asks Jesus about the leadership roles and positions for her two sons. Jesus' reply was, "Whosoever will be great among you, let him be your minister; and whosoever will be chief among you, let him be your servant: Even the Son of man came not to be ministered unto, but to minister, and to give his life a ransom for many" (Matt. 20:26-28). On another occasion Christ said, "He that is greatest among you shall be your servant" (Matt. 23:11).

Two of the examples of servanthood that Christ demonstrated were in situations where he cared for his disciples. Before the Last Supper, Jesus washed the disciples' feet (John 13:1-11). After his resurrection, he prepared breakfast on the beach (John 21:9-14).

The Lord is the model of servant leadership. The following characteristics of a Christ-like servant leader are adapted from Lawrence O. Richards' book, *A Theology of Christian Education.*

Servant relationships The servant leader is one who is among the people, not above the people. The primary emphasis related to servanthood here is on not being in a position of authority, but on being a person who is willing to serve others for the sake of Christ. There should be freedom to share thoughts and feelings in an open climate of spiritual fellowship. Christ asked for this when he prayed, "that they all may be one; as thou, Father, art in me, and I in thee, that they also may be one in us" (John 17:21).

Servant characteristics These qualities include humility, godly living, Christian service, caring, and encouragement.

The Word of God says that the leader is to serve others in a humble, Christ-like way so that the body of Christ is equipped for spiritual service. This means that humility must be the guiding attitude: "he that humbleth himself shall be exalted" (Luke 18:14). Within the context of that humility, leaders are to equip "the saints, for the work of the ministry, for the edifying of the body of Christ" (Eph. 4:12).

Servant model of godly living Leading is to be characterized more by doing for others than by telling others what to do. Peter writes to church leaders that they should not function "as being lords over God's heritage, but being examples to the flock" (I Pet. 5:3). Persons will want to listen to the message of the leader if it is true to the Word of God and is being lived in a Christ-like manner.

Service

This characteristic involves activities that enable a person or group to accomplish the scriptural mandates which are termed "ministry." Christian service can be seen in such activities as teaching a Sunday school class, helping in the church nursery, caring for the sick, and working with a youth group. However, service for Christ is only limited by one's creativity and imagination.

It should be noted that Christ functioned in very specific ways, though service was the thread throughout his life. Realizing that his life was one of service, Jesus said, "I have glorified thee on earth; I have finished the work which thou gavest me to do" (John 17:4) and "I must work the works of him that sent me" (John 9:4). Christ also gave commands to his disciples about the work that they were to accomplish. One of the most specific, and yet all-encompassing challenges, was the commission to "Go ye into all the world, and preach the gospel to every creature" (Mark 16:15).

Through the work of the Holy Spirit and the commitments of Christian leaders, in order to properly reflect Christ's model, there ought to be a sense of industry, accomplishment, and service for Christ associated with all activities of those seeking spiritual growth.

Caring

Caring relationships are seen in activities that promote supportive attitudes between members of a group. Caring leaders help to create warm and loving interpersonal relationships. Christ demonstrated caring in many biblical instances. He said, "These things I command you, that ye love one another" (John 15:17). He related to children with a special kind of compassion, saying, "Suffer little children, and forbid them not, to come unto me: for of such is the kingdom of heaven" (Matt. 19:14). And Jesus referred to himself as "a friend of publicans and sinners" (Matt. 11:19).

Within the area of caring for others, there are also important personal qualities. One of the most important of these qualities is called the fruit of the spirit. The fruit consists of "love, joy, peace, longsuffering, gentleness, goodness, faith, meekness, temperance" (Gal. 5:22,23). In addition, relationships are to reflect faith, hope, and love (I Cor. 13). Of course, the greatest of these is the quality of love.

Delegation

Delegating responsibility involves using and transmitting authority. For delegation to occur, Christians need confidence and trust in one another. They also need to realize that the person who accepts a responsibility is to have the capacity to effectively live up to the implications of that which has been delegated. For example, there would be no basis for appointing someone to be responsible for a youth group if he had no experience working with high school age young people and had little knowledge of Scripture.

As responsibility is delegated, it must be remembered that the Word of God is the Christian's authority base. Leaders must be careful not to make themselves equal with Scripture. Rather, they are servants and stewards who seek to make effective use of their time and talents according to the resources that God has given.

One of the clearest biblical examples of delegation is seen in the advice given by Jethro to his son-in-law, Moses. Jethro observed that Moses was overwhelmed, over-extended, and over-worked by spending all of his time singlehandedly judging the people (Exod. 18:13). In response to the situation, he advised Moses to delegate responsibility as explained in Exodus 18:18-22.

This passage stresses the following important points about delegation.

1. Before being able to delegate correctly, one must be right in relation to God. "Be thou for the people to God-ward" (v. 19).

2. One must be knowledgeable about how the work to be delegated should be performed: "the work that they must do" (v. 20).

3. The persons to be delegated the responsibility should be able, God-fearing, persons of truth, and hating covetousness; their lives must be right with God and with others (v. 21).

New Testament examples of situations where Christ delegated responsibility include John 5:27 and Luke 24:49. In the John passage, the Father gives authority to the Son, "authority to execute judgment also, because he is the Son of man." In the Luke passage, Jesus gives responsibility to the disciples saying, "I send the promise of my Father upon you: but tarry ye in the city of Jerusalem, until ye be endued with power from on high."

Encouragement

Encouragement involves the selection of words to influence the development and spiritual growth of a person. It is also associated with accepting, affirming, and appreciating people.

Principles to consider as a foundation for giving encouragement are set forth in Scripture. First, believers are admonished to be careful when speaking: "Seest thou a man that is hasty in his words? There is more hope of a fool than of him" (Prov. 29:20). Second, believers are to be sensitive when speaking: "The wisdom that is from above is . . . full of mercy" (James 3:17). Third, believers are to be kind when speaking: "A soft answer turneth away wrath" (Prov. 15:1). Simple phrases that are helpful in providing encouragement include: "You really helped me," "Thanks for . . .," and "I appreciate what you are doing."

■ Summary ■

This chapter has provided several guidelines for leadership. And everyone who is seeking to grow and mature as a Christian must become involved in some leadership responsibilities in life and ministry. In every area of leadership responsibility, you will want to view leadership in Christ-like terms when working with others. In every case you will want to follow the servant model of Jesus Christ. In order for you to experience the healthiest growth, your leadership style must always be concerned with doing the tasks of ministry within a climate of loving Christian relationships.

■ Discussion Questions ■

1. What is the definition of leadership?

2. What four areas did Jesus emphasize in regard to leadership?

3. What characteristics should you develop to become an effective leader?

4. Give some examples from Christ's life which demonstrate the importance of servanthood.

5. Why is a caring attitude important to leadership?

6. Why is delegation important?

7. How can you encourage others?

■ Application Activities ■

1. Paraphrase (write in your own words) the following verses about leadership: Matthew 20:26-28 and 23:8-12. What leadership principles can you identify from these verses? What changes would result in the leadership at your church if these verses were taken seriously? What changes would be made in your life if you applied the principles of biblical leadership consistently?

2. Obtain a church bulletin or newsletter. Using these resources, list all of the kinds of Christian service that you see represented. Pick one

activity of which you know little and find out more about it. Identify one area of need and pray about it during the coming week. Decide which area of Christian service is of greatest interest to you and explain why to someone you know.

3. Read Exodus 18:18-22 once again. Think of areas in a group of which you are a member or your church where delegation could make the body of Christ function more effectively. Discuss the concept of delegation with a leader in your church. Ask for examples of effective delegation. If the leader is open, suggest ways delegation could be improved.

■ Bibliography ■

Engstrom, Ted W. and Dayton, Edward R. *The Art of Management for Christian Leaders.* Waco, TX: Word, 1976.

Gangel, Kenneth O. *Leadership for Church Education.* Chicago: Moody, 1970.

_____. *Competent to Lead.* Chicago: Moody, 1974.

Keating, Charles J. *The Leadership Book.* New York: Paulist Press, 1982.

Kilinski, Kenneth and Wofford, Jerry. *Organization and Leadership for the Local Church.* Grand Rapids: Zondervan, 1973.

Richards, Lawrence O. *A Theology of Christian Education.* Grand Rapids: Zondervan, 1975.

Sanders, J. Oswald. *Spiritual Leadership.* Chicago: Moody, 1967.

CONTINUING
YOUR
SPIRITUAL
GROWTH

BEING A LIFELONG LEARNER

12 Growth is a never-ending process in the Christian life. This was true in the lives of such notable biblical personalities as Moses, David, Peter, and Paul, as well as almost every other person in the Scriptures that God used. Even today the phrase, "Please be patient; God is not finished with me yet," is certainly biblically oriented.

The apostle Paul emphatically stressed this point over and over. In Philippians 3:12-14, Paul talks of pressing on and straining for what is ahead; and, in II Timothy 4:7, Paul refers to the Christian life as a race and a fight which continues.

Adult educators often use the term "lifelong learning" when referring to this concept. Although commencement speakers often remind graduates that the granting of their degrees does not indicate an end, but a beginning, this idea seldom makes the impact the speaker desires. However, lifelong learning teaches this exact principle—the formal, school-oriented instruction children and youth receive is the *beginning*, not the end of learning. If our formal schooling has been successful, it will have provided us with the tools to continue learning for the rest of our lives.

■ How does one become involved in such learning? ■

Adults learn in many ways. In fact, some research has indicated that adults may learn differently and have differing learning styles. To provide for such differences, lifelong learning possibilities are often divided into formal and non-formal learning.

Formal learning

Formal Christian adult education is increasing rapidly in popularity and interest and is most often thought of as structured classroom learning experiences. Following are some of the most common possibilities:

Adult Sunday School In the context of the local church, this is an excellent opportunity for adult learning. Since adults have varying needs and interests, many churches provide elective classes on different topics and subjects. Adults select the class which will be most valuable to them in their Christian lives and growth. At the same time, they determine personal goals for participating in the class which may be slightly different from the goals of the course but will guide their own involvement in the class.

Evening Bible Institute Individual churches or several churches in a community often cooperate to develop an adult Bible institute. These programs usually meet one night a week and often include course offerings in Bible, doctrine, and lay ministry topics. Some form of adult education credit leading to a certificate or diploma is often offered as well.

Colleges and Seminaries As the most populous age in our world moves from adolescence to adult, the age level of the typical college student is changing. In the early 1980s the number of persons in all the non-adult age groups in North America decreased (except 0-5 year olds). In contrast to this, the 25-44 year olds increased by 10%. Those 65 years of age and older increased by 7.2%. By the 1990s the demographics for the 25-44 year olds will have soared to a 45% increase while those 65 years and older will increase 25%. In light of these figures, Christian colleges and seminaries are providing both non-degree and degree programs geared especially for such adults. This includes courses at convenient times during the day, evening school classes, correspondence school courses, Saturday "weekend college," summer school sessions, with fee structures more appropriate to part-time students.

Adult Bible Studies Perhaps the most popular phenomenon in Christian adult education in the last decade is the adult Bible study. Sometimes these programs meet in homes, sometimes in the church or another setting, but the goals are always the same—to provide opportunity to study and discuss God's Word in an informal setting, to apply biblical truths to daily lives, and to fellowship with one another. Many varieties of Bible studies also exist. These range from those especially for ladies, men, couples, singles, and systematic Bible study or are evangelistic in their recruitment goals. Adult Bible studies fulfill an important growth need of every Christian; that is, to have the opportunity to systematically study the Bible in the fellowship and support of fellow believers.

Seminars, Conferences, Workshops Although not as prevalent now, within the last decade seminars, conferences, and workshops for Christian adults have had tremendous success. Leadership and teaching skills, marriage and family insights, and theology and Bible content areas are popular topics at seminars and workshops. Denominational and preaching conferences are also popular for adults. However, to achieve the full benefit of these meetings, specific personal goals must be determined prior to attending. And, plans should be formulated and recorded at the conclusion of the seminar, conference, or workshop for putting into practice what has been learned. Ideally, several individuals who attended the same conference will later meet to discuss personal reactions and applications.

In the final analysis, adult learning is an individual endeavor. Although each of these formal learning opportunities includes interaction with other adults, the full benefit of each learning experience will only be realized as individual adults determine personal learning goals prior to participating and make plans for application after involvement in the learning experience.

Non-formal learning

A phase of lifelong learning often overlooked is non-formal learning— the independent learning opportunities all adults participate in nearly every day. Whether it's seeking an answer to a problem through conversations, reading, or study, or a more structured independent learning project, you are constantly involved in informal learning. Following are some examples:

Personal Devotions/Bible Study Whether it's through the use of a daily devotional guide, a study of a biblical or theological topic or question, or studying a book of the Bible, personal Bible study is one of the most significant learning experiences contributing to your spiritual growth. To help organize these learning experiences, you might keep a notebook to record what you learn during your personal Bible study and devotions.

Sermons Sermons can be excellent learning experiences. Whether it be the pastor's Sunday morning, evening, or midweek message or a sermon heard on a radio or television broadcast, these can be good opportunities for adult learning. This can be especially true when the message corresponds with your personal Bible study. Taking sermon notes in your Bible or a separate notebook is a good reinforcement technique. It is also helpful to discuss the sermon (with the preacher, if possible) and make plans for applying its message to your spiritual life.

Reading Books, magazines, and journals for Christian adults abound. Since you control the subject choice and the time committed to reading, this approach has high practical appeal. Regularly reading a journal or magazine of personal and spiritual interest will be helpful to your walk with the Lord. Every growing Christian adult should plan a book reading pattern which meets particular spiritual needs on a regular basis.

Adult Learning Projects Almost every day, adults are involved in learning, whether it be researching an idea in a library or asking questions of an individual more knowledgeable in a particular area. However, in doing this you should determine what it is you desire to learn and then devise a course of action to achieve that learning.

Contract Learning Though more commonly seen in formal adult educational situations, learning can become personal and individualized in non-formal learning through the use of contract learning. In this approach, each adult selects a topic or question of interest and then determines a specific learning plan to follow and what the expected result will be of his or her learning. In a non-formal setting, contract learning is simply you contracting with yourself for content, learning outcomes, and those awards you grant yourself as a consequence.

■ What subject areas should you pursue? ■

Growing spiritually is a lifelong process which will only be complete when you see Christ face-to-face. You, therefore, should make growing to spiritual maturity a lifetime goal so that you can live your life for Christ. Following are some areas which should be considered in lifelong learning:

Bible knowledge
The Bible is the believer's textbook for life and, by virtue of this, is perhaps the most important element in lifelong learning. An increased knowledge and understanding of the Scriptures should be a major goal of every adult believer. Those books of the Bible which are least known and understood should be studied more. At the beginning of each year you should determine your personal goals for your own study of the Scriptures and plan a learning strategy to meet those goals during the year.

Theology and practical Christian living
A proper understanding of the scriptural teachings on the ministries of Christ, biblical doctrines, and how to live the Christian life is also very important. No adult believer should be reluctant to become involved in a study of scriptural theology. Only as you know what the Bible truly teaches can you talk with non-believers, understand the errors in heretical and cultic teachings, and live the Christian life to the fullest.

Practical ministry
Each adult believer is gifted with abilities from the Holy Spirit for the edification of the church and fellow believers. These gifts and abilities, however, must be further developed for their fullest and best use—which is bringing glory to God. You, therefore, should be involved in church training classes to increase your ability to minister effectively. This may include instruction in teaching, leading a person to Christ, counseling, visitation, or other ministries, as well as foundational subject areas.

■ Putting it all together ■
Every adult learning experience is beneficial. However, for adult learning to have an impact on the life, ministry, and spiritual growth of adults, the various experiences must be organized in a way that will best suit the individual needs and goals of each adult believer. Following are several principles you might use in organizing an individual learning plan to provide for satisfying lifelong learning.

Determine your personal goals
Any learning program requires a specific direction and objectives. Your individual adult learning plan is no different. These goals should be based primarily on your needs. For example, you might identify some areas in which you would like to improve in the coming months and years. Or you may identify some areas in which you would like increased knowledge such as ministry or daily living challenges you will be facing in the near future. These personal needs all lead to the specific goals

you will establish for learning and, thus, should be recorded for later evaluation.

Determine learning experiences which will meet your goals

Next, you will want to determine which formal and informal learning experiences will best achieve the goals you stated. Perhaps you will want to participate in various church study groups, a Sunday school class, or other formal adult learning experiences, or maybe it will be necessary to achieve your learning goals through non-formal means. Matching your goals to the best learning experiences to attain them is a necessary second step to achieving your goals.

Organize selected learning experiences into your plan

If specific learning experiences are scheduled for each month or quarter of the year which will contribute to achieving your individual learning objectives, use a calendar to schedule those learning opportunities you choose to participate in throughout the year. Organizing your time is called time management and is crucial to accomplishing spiritual growth.

Determine how you will know when your goals have been met

Are there specific skills or outcomes which should be evidenced at the conclusion of the learning plan? You will want to identify specific areas of knowledge or behavior changes which should be enhanced at the end of the learning experience. In some way, you need to be clear concerning how you will know when the learning is complete and the goals have been met. These are called measurable objectives.

As the learning experiences work together to accomplish specific purposes, real growth and development will result. In many ways, developing an individual learning plan is the key to realizing the true potential of lifelong learning.

■ Summary ■

Growth is a continual process for the Christian. Every biblical personality whom God used experienced this continual learning process which is emphasized especially in the writings of the apostle Paul.

Opportunities for lifelong learning abound for you, as a spiritually-growing adult believer, whether through formal or non-formal means. However, only as you prepare an individual learning plan will you realize the impact on these learning opportunities in achieving the spiritual growth that is most honoring to Christ.

■ Discussion Questions ■

1. Investigate the available formal learning opportunities that would be of interest to you. List those that have potential to you in the next two years.
2. Investigate the available informal learning opportunities that would be of interest to you. List them as you did above.

3. Why should wider Bible knowledge be a priority goal in lifelong learning? Regarding Bible knowledge, what personal strategy would best serve you in achieving such goals?

4. Why is practical ministry an important part of spiritual growth?

5. In what areas of ministry could you best use your gifts?

6. Why is it important to have an organized plan for lifelong learning?

■ Application Activity ■

Take a sheet of paper and draw the following chart.

Personal Goals	Learning Experiences	Outcomes
1.		
2.		
3.		

Next to the numbers, write in a specific personal goal that reflects a true need that you feel. Then, under "Learning Experiences," write which learning experiences (formal or non-formal) will best help you acheive that goal. Finally, under "Outcomes" write a *measurable* means to evaluate when you will have met your personal goal.

Note: The best way to identify a measurable objective is to simply ask, "What will I be *doing* when I have met my goal?" That is a tangible behavior that you can identify and measure. Place a time reference as to when you expect this outcome to be visible.

Continue the process for each personal goal you list.

■ Bibliography ■

Aslanian, Carol B. and Brickell, Henry M. *Americans in Transition.* Princeton, NJ: College Entrance Examination Board, 1980.

Steinbron, Melvin J. *Can the Pastor do it Alone?* Ventura, CA: Regal Books, 1987.

Sweeting, George W. *You Can Climb Higher.* Nashville: Thomas Nelson, 1985.

268.0715
B8 25

CONCLUSION

In this short text, by exploring how growth occurs inwardly and through ministry, we have tried to provide a sure foundation as well as adequate scope for your spiritual growth. We have also shared what we feel are our society's implications on your growth pilgrimage.

The authors have tried to lift spiritual growth up to the light, like a fresh-cut diamond, to reveal its many facets. We concluded that there is no special formula that will insure spiritual growth. As a plant needs the right soil and environment to develop, these ingredients are also important to spiritual growth.

The soil is the Word of God, the Bible. Scripture will always be the best nutritional source for our roots. Thus, we must again and again go back to the Bible for a proper feeding of our spiritual roots.

The environment is also critical. One would quickly equate the environment to the church where we are constantly nurtured and cultivated. But that is only partially true. Along with the church, the world needs to be included in our environment. Although we don't need the world's values, we do need the world as an environment in which to blossom and bear fruit. To grow spiritually both church and the world are needed.

As the mighty oak required many storms to build its extensive root system and tough bark, believers also need the world to develop and strengthen their faith. For as the world reacts, rebuffs, and challenges our faith, a strange phenomenon occurs—we grow. Church history has always shown that the church of Christ grew toward spiritual maturity when it was under oppression.

We now realize that attempting to live for Christ in monastic seclusion is, at best, counter-productive. Exposure to the world brings with it a special environment which produces spiritual growth. Whether that environment produces growth or not depends on how we use it.

This world environment is also necessary since it is where we can share the good news of the gospel with those who are in darkness and sin. With 5 billion persons on this planet, our personal declaration of faith is essential to the evangelical mission the Lord has called us to perform. It also is a curious phenomenon that when we actively express our faith to others, unique spiritual growth occurs. Some theologians feel that the greatest stimulant to our spiritual growth is sharing our faith in Christ.

One of a believer's greatest joys is seeing his/her life multiplied through sharing Christ with others. Being able to multiply your Christian life in this way surely brings glory to God. This is our prayer for you.